Mario Botta
Architectural Poetics

First published in the United Kingdom in 2001 by
Thames & Hudson Ltd, 181A High Holborn
London WC1V 7QX

www.thamesandhudson.com

British Library Cataloguing-in-Publication Data
A catalogue record for this book is available
from the British Library

ISBN 0-500-28293-5

Printed and bound in Italy

On the cover:
Front: Villa facade, Bernareggio, Italy. Photo Pino Musi.
Back: Gerbio Residences, Monte Carasso, Bellinzona, Switzerland.
Photo Filippo Simonetti.

Mario Botta
Architectural Poetics

Irena Sakellaridou

 Thames & Hudson

Logic of Form, Richness of Meaning

Architecture gives form to space. During the thirty-five years of his impressive career, Mario Botta has indeed given form to space, and meaning to form. Both in his homeland and abroad, all over the world, his buildings assert their powerful configuration. Their clarity of outline defines a figure immediately perceived and understood, its meaning lying in the longing for the spiritual and the ethical. His architecture is both recognized by the layman and acclaimed by the critic. His numerous buildings, countless publications, exhibitions and awards have brought him international fame. Working in his office in Lugano, Switzerland, Botta has become a renowned public figure.

Throughout his long career Botta has built and experimented with a wide range of architectural typologies, from the symbolic heights of the cathedral to the mystical atmosphere of the chapel, from the contemporary temple of the museum to the iconic immediacy of the service station. He has designed housing and office buildings, villas and public spaces, theater sets, furniture and wristwatches.

Mario Botta is an architect. His architecture gives form to space; a form that is incisive, distinct and meaningful. His architecture is exact and ordered. There is no space for coincidence, no room allowed for arbitrary decisions. His architecture conserves the memory of the stone wall, the reminiscence of the primary form. His forms search for the eternal and not the ephemeral, for the long-lasting and not the transient. While the density of their meaning carries the memory of the archaic, his architecture is nevertheless modern. However, it does not hesitate to acknowledge the overriding power of symmetry, to explore the expressiveness of material, playing with its decorative richness.

For Botta, form is the medium. He does not talk about his forms, about the primacy of his volumes, or the solidity of his walls. He does, however, describe the relation of his buildings to the site, the landscape and the city. He points to the importance of natural light and its relationship with the cycle of seasons and time. He describes the need for a point of reference on the inside, for a transitional space on the outside. He does not, however, talk about his forms, for his forms are what he works with, the material he uses to give shape to his search for the essence of architecture. His forms are the artist's paint, the sculptor's mould, the architect's means for making the boundless defined and the unrealized concrete.

The house enjoys a privileged place in Botta's oeuvre. In the early years of his career, it was through a series of houses that his architectural idiom, his personal style was developed. In his own words, "The home is the number one item for the architect's attention. It embraces the idea of the habitat and the domestic and thus of the organization of man's living space; the idea of a relationship with a context and the existing territory; the memory of the primitive home; and the shelter that meets one of man's basic needs. In developing this theme, I would like these three moments to remain always in mind, so that the architecture is the faithful mirror of the possibilities and the hopes of its own time. I would like the home always to be a product of man in harmony with cosmic values, with the solar cycle, the passing of the seasons and of time. However, if the theme of the home is that of shelter," he continues, "the theme of the church is the theme of silence, by means of which one can explore the yearning for spirituality."[1]

In the process of shifting from the house to the church, from one project to the next, creativity remains constant, vividly invigorating the given and giving form to the new. If, in formal terms, a house is a hollowed-out primary solid, with a characteristic front, with a symmetry that organizes volume, elevations and plan and with an interior where logical distinctions of notions become formally expressed,[2] then, in order to express the church such rules are transformed. Like the house of man, the house of God is an object that stands autonomously, strongly rooted to the ground. However, the church also becomes the place where the collective space for contemplation and the dynamic upward movement towards the divine meet. It becomes a symbol of the contact of man with nature, a symbol of the existence of the sacred in the everyday and the profane. Distinctions between the external world and the internal, between suspension and movement of gaze, between the sacred and the profane become dyadic pairs of notions which are implicitly integrated through the rules that underlie the composition. In the church, form and meaning become united in a powerful whole.[3]

Moving from the house to the church, from shelter to silence, is like moving from the man-made to the spiritual, from the search for order that would mediate between site, life cycle, space and form, to order that transgresses human limitations in search of everlasting values of the spirit. Like a paradigm of how his idiom evolved, the house and the church signify the journey from order within the artificial to a search for symbolism of the timeless, from the wish for architectural order to the longing for meaning. Botta's architecture, deeply rooted in fundamental values, in values both ethical and eternal, is architecture of reason and of feeling.

The themes that inform Botta's architecture are ties that connect and backbones that support, common threads that bind one building to the next. Themes like the primary solid and the wall; the eminence of the front; the light coming from above; the point of reference; the site. These themes are explored again and again for they are the tools which make reason and meaning concrete, which fulfill the wish for architectural space and the desire for form.

In the architecture of Mario Botta, volume is defined *a priori*. It is not the result of the aggregation of different parts. Neither is it an outcome, an end product. It is designed, conceived beforehand. Volumetric definition is a starting point in the adventure of architectural design. The building needs to have an identity that can be read. The outline of its volume plays this role. It makes the building a representation of an autonomous object that stands in the landscape, calm and self-contained. However, the building is not indifferent to its surroundings, and in its dialogue with them it does not hesitate to look different and assert its presence.

Volume is imbedded with signification. Its primary form will not be bent, distorted or deformed; it can be transformed, but its origin will always remain clear. The square, or the triangle, the rectangle or the cylinder; the variations are many. However, shape is not what is important, for the constitution of form is not a matter of shape. There might be a preference for the cylinder, but the compactness of its signification, its potential as a symbolic form gives it a privileged status among the other primary solids. What is hidden behind the shape and what defines its formal constitution are, instead, more important to its selection.

It does not necessarily have to be only one volume. Usually, however, there is one, main form-giver. Smaller volumes need to be distinguished from the main one; the rectangle is distinct from the cylinder, the straight line from the curved. When there are more volumes, their coming together will follow exact rules. Axes of symmetry need to be employed. The power of the message will not be deterred by asymmetrical variations. Symmetry will be the overall rule of order.

The *primary solid* does not remain intact. Subtractions from its mass create play between positive and negative space. Subtractions create transitional spaces, an intermediary between the inside and the outside. The volume is hollowed out to let the outside become part of it, to give shelter to the exterior and bring it close to the interior. The volume cannot extend beyond its limits, for its limits are what give it identity. This is not architecture of non-defined edges, of limitless space. Instead of extending, the volume can include, envelope and contain. The limits between the inside and the outside will always be exact, defined and ordered.

If volume speaks about the three-dimensional, external boundary takes up the issue of the two-dimensional. However, in Botta's architecture this two-dimensional surface does not just form a plane. It is a *wall*, not an abstract notion; it is real, has a material nature, emphasizes the solid. Being the boundary of a volume, it does not stand on its own. It always wraps around the volume. It might be a skin, but it has mass. Could it be attributed to Romanesque memories of the solid wall, or to the stone walls of the vernacular of Botta's home region? What existed before and of old, can still be translated into the new, for architecture works with memory.

The wall of Mario Botta is not ephemeral; it has duration. Material plays an important role, gives the wall its texture and communicates its solidity. The cladding, in brick or stone, covers the wall all around. Protrusions and recesses, turns in brick layers, shadows and illumination and alternations of strips with different colored stones, accentuate its solid presence. Later on, stone becomes even more expressive; it gives the wall a form, not as a cladding any longer, but as a mould that shapes it in total precision.

The surface is emptied out at the base, to be completed at the top. The edge remains almost continuous, so that the reading of the volume is intact. The wall accepts perforations ordered by the overall rules. The missing parts become glass surfaces, usually in retreat. The windows are never stated, never designed for their own sake. They are only necessary perforations on the surface, their rhythmical repetition intensifying the reading of the solid wall.

The building has a face; a silent front. Silent does not mean in-expressiveness. Expression in architecture should not be loud, for architecture speaks the language of silence. The building has *a front* that becomes its face with which to look at the world. Always directed towards the view when in an open landscape, or towards the street when in a city, the front, in the form of an elaborate facade, becomes the image of the building itself.

The front, even in the very early examples of Botta's architecture, is carefully designed. Subtractions from the mass of the primary solid, glass surfaces in recess, vertical cuts and skylights, become elements in a composition ordered by symmetry, in a powerful logical relation that sets rules of similarity and spatial relations at the same time. Gradually the facade becomes more and more detailed. It moves forward, it bends, its material becomes more elaborate, emphasizing its difference as an entity amidst a universe of undifferentiated elements. The facade becomes a face proper. Sometimes it even dares to move beyond ordered symmetrical abstraction to play with anthropomorphic allusions. Then again, having explored its possibilities, frontality becomes an issue of volume once more. Volumetric composition acquires directionality, gains a front.

With the solidity of the wall and the massiveness of the volume, the transparency of the roof becomes an element of surprise. Perforations in the wall are only a necessity. The *celebration of light* has always to do with the way the roof opens up to the sky and lets natural light flood into the interior. The changing of the seasons, the shadows and colors of the sky and the passing of time are part of the architecture. The use of natural light becomes symbolic. The shelter cannot isolate from nature. Light reminds us of the cycle of seasons and life. If the solidity of the wall dares to hint at eternal time, at the ever existing and unchangeable, the relation of the building to light speaks about the ever-changing and ephemeral nature of existence.

This element, which gives spatial quality to his first buildings, is exalted to the point of becoming the main design feature in Botta's churches. The silence of the sacred place can only be broken by the explosion of light. The solid wall and the transparent roof become a dyadic notion that condenses all meaning. Where the solid stands for the man-made, the transparent stands for man's desire to aspire to something greater than his own limited existence. Life and nature, time and change are shown by the antithesis between the solid and the transparent. Pregnant in meaning and yet so simple and direct, the bringing together of these two notions elevates space and form-making into architectural poetics.

While volumetric composition and the articulation of a front speak about the reading of the exterior, the clarity of the interior and its spatial structure are equally important to Botta. The desire to read the outline of the building as a sign becomes transformed into a need for clear spatial organization, the desire to be able to grasp it all at once. The external boundary shapes, the interior with as little interruption as possible. With its continuity and clear geometry, it keeps the reference to the primary volume intact. Movement and experience of the space are guided by a continuous visual field. Our gaze is allowed to explore the space, to follow the contours of the boundary, to concentrate on a point of interest, to wander around. Geometry has a role to play in the reading of space. Axes of symmetry, emphasized corners and the symmetrical ordering of walls and subtractions are means by which composition gives meaning to the interior.

Intelligibility of the interior need not remain tacit. A *point of reference* is introduced to orient and guide. A point of reference, usually a void that visually connects the different floors, has its role enhanced by the ample light coming from above. The void amplifies the spatial sense; the vertical and the horizontal expansion of space unite. If the front facade concentrates meaning, standing as a sign for the whole building, the focal point of interest in the interior is the dense expression of spatial organization. The void becomes more and more significant in the composition. It gradually gains volumetric definition; it becomes a three-dimensional element in itself. Then, in Botta's churches, the void takes possession of the whole space; space becomes transformed into a grand void that opens to the sky. At other times, the point of reference is moved to the exterior, is even transformed into negative space, into a courtyard.

And then there is the *site*. The site is, for Botta, full of potential. It is a context and a topography, a physical reality and a geographical situation, a necessary constraint and a welcome inspiration. For him, "A work of architecture is a synthesis of two things: an architect's thought—abstract or ideological, as the case might be—and physical reality. This reality is, first and foremost, a geographical situation."[4]

Instead of 'building on a site', the building 'builds the site'. When in open landscape, the building stands out and signifies its existence with its solid volume and ordered geometry. By either emphasizing the vertical dimension or extending along the horizontal, its mass is delineated by the geometry of its volume and its elaborate and disciplined front relates to the view. When in the city, the front takes account of street elevations and responds without sacrificing its desire for an independent presence. Even in its assertion, the elaboration of the volume responds with delicate gestures. It follows street lines and takes account of the urban fabric. It diminishes its size in order not to upset existing scale. It creates a limit with its linearity or a point of reference with its primary geometry. It hides its mass, placing it underground to leave space for the existing, or it boldly asserts its presence by setting up dialogue with a landmark. When on a street corner, it addresses this corner appropriately. When on a large scale, it opens up its courtyard to make space for the public realm and invites the city into the building. The city will always be there, as a context and underlying reference, and the building relates and responds.

Mario Botta's narrative is structured, with content and form in close relation. His text is controlled, measured and weighted. And yet, syntactic order does not limit, but liberates; does not confine, but enriches with its potential. It does not remain silent; it speaks about the adventures of space, it tells the story of form. What gives Botta's architecture its strong identity is an internal logic that guides and underlies formal expression. His first buildings have already introduced his themes. These themes combine, interweave, and influence all aspects of the building, they set architectural rules that order the formation of the volume, the elevations and the plan, defining the way the building will be looked at from afar and will face the world. All this defines his logic of form. Rules in interrelation create an *intensive compositional structure*, by virtue of which everything relates to the other and everything obeys the overall order.[5] It is a structure that is stable and yet in a continuous state of flux between the creative search for the new and the transformation of what has already been explored. It is an internal logic of bringing everything together, *logic of oneness*, a logic that intensifies the reading of the whole and attributes dense meaning to the form. It is a compositional idiom that allows for creative transformations from one building to another, transformations, which bring forward a different theme and suggest a different reading. Rules may become autonomous, but they do not upset the stability of the deep structure, for this structure is deeply rooted in the essential, firmly based on the substantial.

By exploring the expressive potential of his space and form, never ceasing to experiment with them, Botta continuously invents what is a strong possibility in the vast universe of unrealized architectural probability. He investigates the limits of his discipline and lets his intuition be guided by order. He interrogates the existing and carries forward memories of the old. He shapes the new and designs limits for space through boundaries and clear outlines, for Mario Botta is an architect and his architectural poetics are the poetics of space and form.

Thirty-three buildings, three stage-sets and numerous designed objects constitute only a small sample of an explosive talent, of a productive life of over thirty-five years. This presentation will attempt to follow the steps of time. However, beneath chronological order lies an order of a different kind; order that speaks about the formation of an architectural language that is distinct and personal, and yet universally recognized and cherished. The search for order in the first period will give way to the creative transformations of maturity. Form will become more and more expressive and symbolic; scale will vary with the large and the small competing for attention. What is common and what is different, what is new and how it relates to what is already there, what is introduced earlier on and explored later, will be the focus of the following chapters. Before attention is paid to each project, an overall review of broad stages will introduce the work. However, chronological order will be used only as a necessary formulation, for creativity cannot be confined by order of this type.

Chapter One

Search for Order

Single-family house in Stabio

A compositional idiom does not evolve in just one day. It takes time. However, traits of the elements that were to become so characteristic in the architecture of Mario Botta were evident even from the very beginning. Three buildings of this period are presented here—examples that condense the explorations of that time and illustrate the important themes. The issue of the site underlies all three of them. While the Middle School in Morbio Inferiore (1972-1977) deals with the "building of a site," the Library at the Capuchin Convent (1976-1979) also explores the same relationship. This time, however, instead of using a strong linear element to stand in antithesis with the undifferentiated character of the area, as in the case of the School, or instead of creating a point of reference as in the House at Stabio (1980-1981), the Library hides its mass underground. The use of natural light from above to provide orientation, and the reading of the external boundary leaving the interior as unobstructed as possible are themes that are explored in the Library and also appear in the School and the House. The emptying out of volume, the definition of the primary solid by restoring the continuity of the surface at the top, the subtraction of mass in order to create transitional space, geometrical clarity, and symmetrical ordering are all present. This is a phase of invention and experimentation. Themes that will continue to permeate Mario Botta's architecture from now on have already been introduced. Their interrelationship is effected. Their ordering into a structure is explored. The search for order that underlies this early period is not a mannerism. It is a search that delves deep into the essence of architecture and explores the logic of architectural composition.

Middle School in Morbio Inferiore

Ticino, Switzerland, 1972-1977

The school, one of the first public buildings designed by Mario Botta, extends gracefully in linear form within a rural landscape, at the foot of a hillside close to the towns of Chiasso and Balerna. A prizewinner in an architectural competition, it shows traits of what was to become a significant element in the architect's expression. The building is not simply an object placed on a site; it actually transforms, it "builds" this site. Its form is a striking gesture that gives new meaning to the landscape. The austerity and power of its linear volume contrast with the degradation of the urban environment. Sitting on the site, seemingly indifferent to its surroundings, it creates a strong point of reference. Like all Mario Botta's "mature" buildings, this one is a true landmark in the landscape. "With respect to its surroundings," Botta recalls, "the architectural design affords an opportunity not to construct *on a site*, but to construct *that site*, so that the architecture can join the new geographical configuration in a direct link with the qualities of history and of memories peculiar to the place, in token of the aspirations and values of contemporary culture."[1]

Covering a total surface of about 15,000 square meters, the linear volume is broken into separate units. These units consist of a set of classrooms and a great portal that creates a powerful break in the mass of the building, linking the serene landscape in front of the school with the woods at the back. This design feature is, however, of much greater significance. In a subtle deviation from the expected, what is read in the floorplan as a unit of four classrooms is divided in volume into two by the great portal. The units one identifies in the plan are not the same as those one encounters in the volume. Upon reaching the ground, the mass is emptied. In the middle of each unit the building becomes almost transparent. At the top, the boundary that shapes the mass becomes complete once more. The volume can now be read as such. Edges of surfaces, vertical and horizontal, bound this mass. The distance between each unit is kept to a minimum. Repetition of *many* is only meant to signify the unity of *one*. Linearity is reinstated.

This is not a building with centrality. A strong formal element, an interior walkway, constitutes a long corridor with classrooms on each side and forms the main route for circulation, which is brightly illuminated by skylights on the roof. This "backbone" in the building, which forms a linear core, gathers public activity and offers views of all three floors through the use of voids, staircases and open corridors. Skylights create a series of triangular forms, which, in their rhythmic repetition, become one of the fundamental formal elements in the building. The play with negative space, internal voids, and light, creates reference points for the readability of the spatial structure. The school exhibits a kind of brutalism, evident in the reinforced concrete texture of its facades. Color is used on the concrete of some of the interior walls. A stone figure by sculptor Giuseppe Selmoni lying gracefully on the grass surprises and contrasts with the austerity of the built form. A small open amphitheater, the entrance building, and the rectangle of the gymnasium complete the composition.

Eastern side of the building facing the woods   On the following pages: the sequence of
and the hill   blocks facing the front lawn

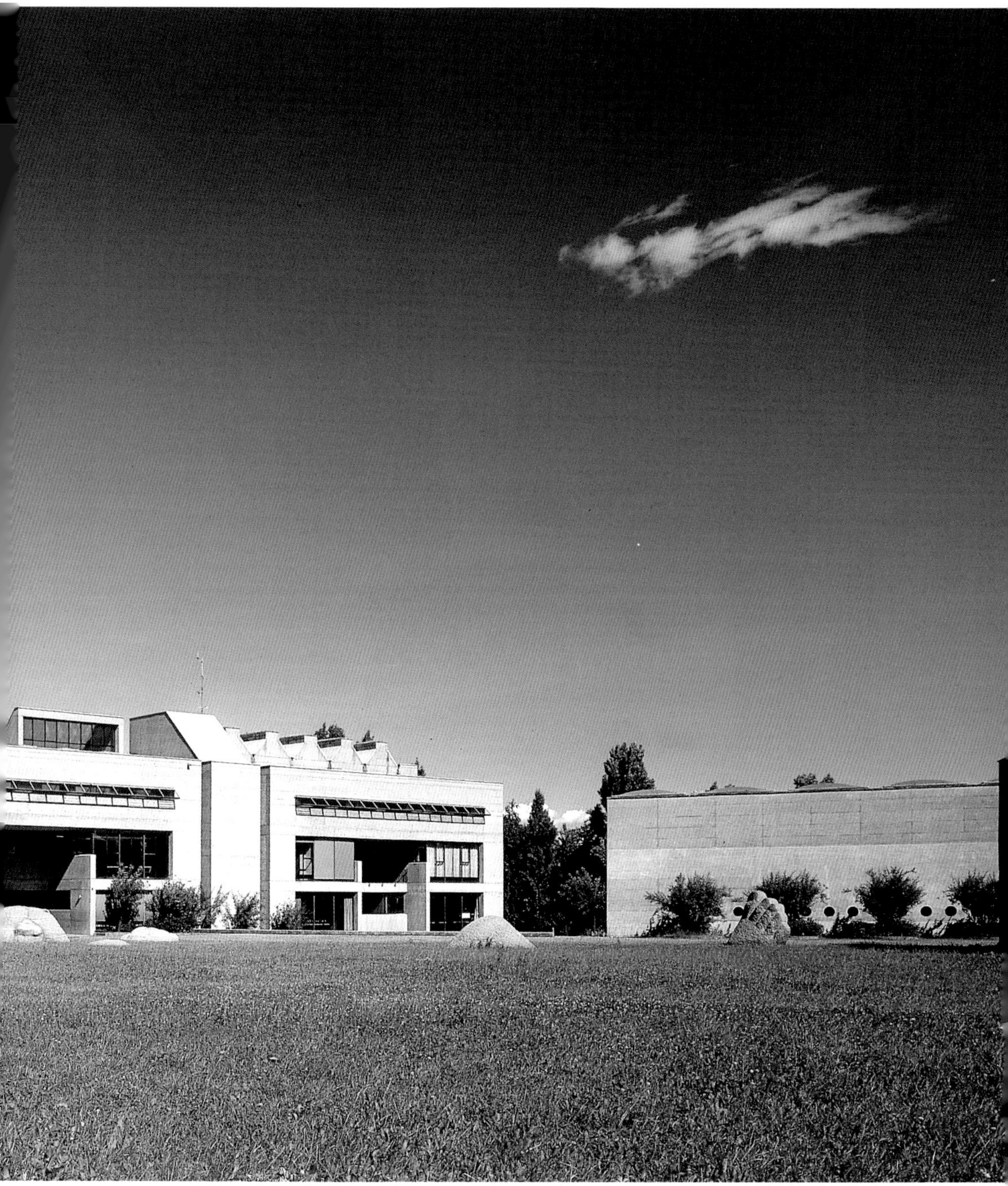

This is architecture of mass. Surface is only the means to delineate this mass. What is, however, to become the recognizable architectural language of Mario Botta is already present. Clarity of geometry, massiveness of form, careful emptying out of the primary volume, linearity of the volume and the subtle breaking of it, as well as the use of light, become powerful elements in its composition. The building does not present a face to the external world like the architect's later works. It addresses the world, instead, by the overall constitution of its mass. By constructing a site through its form, the building can communicate its relationship with the landscape, about the presence and permanence of the architectural object.

Facing page: the central interior corridor with staircases connecting the various levels crosses all the blocks and is lit by large skylights

On this page: perspective sketch and interior view of the library

Library at the Capuchin Convent

Lugano, Switzerland, 1976-1979

An underground building is a building with no facades. Its mass is hidden; it cannot be read in the conventional manner. Partial facades, skylights, and extrusions from the ground demarcate its presence. While manipulations of the mass and the external surface delineate the existence of a building above ground, in an underground building, the interior void formed by its concave surface becomes important. A building underground gives form to an excavation, gives shape to a void. It cannot face the world; nor can it make a statement by an obvious presence, therefore the power of empty space, the play with surface, variations in height, and the presence of a single unitary concept that holds the whole together, become even more important in the case of the subterranean. Since immediate relation with the ground is reversed, the relation with the sky is that much more intense.

In addition, when the underground building is a library, reading internal spatial order, that is, "orienting yourself" and finding your way through, or making distinctions between the public and the more specific areas, become significant issues that set prerequisites for the composition. The treatment of surface also gains priority. Surface, this single form-giving element in a building, which has lost its emphasis on the external, becomes an element that gives more than just shape. When the possibility of communicating with the external is diminished, texture plays a role in giving meaning to the internal. An underground building is, thus, a building of reversals in terms of manipulation of mass, surface and light.[2] This is exactly the case in the public library by Mario Botta.

The underground library, an extension of the Capuchin Convent in Lugano, rests serenely in a vineyard. Covering an area of 900 square meters, it is also used for seminars as well as for small exhibitions in the park. A series of windows that overlook the town, forming vertical slits in an austere concrete wall, and the triangular skylight structure are the only indications of the building hidden under the ground. A long rectilinear volume houses the collections, while a hexagon doubled in height forms the spacious reading area, and these two areas are connected by an intermediate link. A bright entrance, an atrium in the vaulted space of the old building invites the visitor to explore what is hidden underneath. Entry is by means of the mezzanine, which opens out through a large void to the main floor where the reading room is situated, while the skylight on the roof delineates the axis.

Concrete walls, with an interior finish of white brick, shape the reading room. Concrete surfaces create sharp edges for the mezzanine floor and the skylight and contrast with the repetition of the modular structure of the ceilings. The alternating geometry creates tension. Perspective draws the eye toward the top, directing its gaze to the sky above. What is hidden underneath needs to maintain its relation to the sky. Surface, giving shape to the concave, will play this important role: material and texture will become potent signifiers.

The reading room with the deep vertical incision
in the wall showing the internal masonry and
indicating the axis of the underground volume

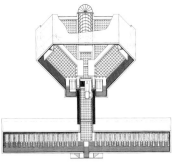

At the entrance level access is provided for
the first reading-reference area.
Below: axonometric.

Facing page: library reading room with large
central skylight

A deep vertical incision in the wall, exactly on the axis of symmetry formed by the skylight, reveals the material underneath. It speaks about separation of materials, about material layers formed one on top of the other, about layers of multiple meaning signified by syntactical order. The texture of the internal surface, formal order and materiality, light and shadow, openness and enclosure, all take part in the overall composition. The Capuchin Library is indeed a place for meditation, filled with serenity and calm, a place for introversion, for thought and contemplation, a mystical place that rests peacefully among the vineyards.

House in Stabio

(Casa Rotonda) Ticino, Switzerland, 1980-1981

As the first of his round buildings, this house enjoys a distinctive place in the series of Mario Botta's private houses. The typology of the cylinder celebrates the autonomous form of the building, which enables it to stand within the landscape and face the view, without having to enter into a dialogue with its indifferent surroundings. Mario Botta recalls: "The intention was to avoid comparison or contrast of the building with the surrounding structures and to establish a spatial rapport with the landscape and the distant horizon. The house is a hint of a tower, an object that defines and outlines itself. The cylindrical volume avoids the need for facades that would have entailed a confrontation with neighboring houses. Such construction is rationalized by the space it occupies between the earth (to which it is anchored at its perimeter) and the sky (to which it is open vertically through its lantern).[3]

The building is a primary solid—a cylinder. Gradually the volume is hollowed out to create transitional spaces: spaces between the inside and the outside. Negative space, created by the hollowing out of the mass, has its own form. What is subtracted remains equally ordered, following the overall rules of the constitution of mass. Subtractions at the front imply an axis of symmetry; a negative axis is implied by delineating absence. Another axis, realized this time at the back, takes form through the vertical element of the staircase. The primary volume might not originally have a front and a back, its shape denies orientation and reacts to directionality. The house, however, does possess a front. A rule of *frontality*, imposing different treatment on a front facade for the building with which to face the world, underlies even a cylindrical volume which, by definition, resists it. The external boundary delineates the cylindrical mass, but while parts might be subtracted, its edges remain continuous. Absence of perforation, apart from the large glass surfaces created, where subtraction from the volume takes place, as well as continuity in the external boundary, contribute to the reading of the primary solid.

For the interior, a clear distinction is drawn between night and day areas, which are allocated to different floors on entry to the ground floor. The first floor is the day zone, while the second is the night zone. A large opening in the volume creates an internal void that connects all floors visually, and a skylight floods the space with light. The double structural walls are made from cement blocks. Thus, a material that was much in use at the time the house was built, is here to remain: plain, with no plaster. The powerful form and the distinct geometry are emphasized by the clarity of structure. The texture of material enriches the overall constitution of the volume, allowing the light to play across the surface and accentuate it.

It is not only the use of the cylinder that makes this house significant in the development of Mario Botta's idiom. It might be the first time the architect chooses to work with the cylindrical form, but it is what underlies the form and shape that is even more important. It is what constitutes the logic of formal composition that makes this house one of the "canonic"[4] houses in the development of his

architectural language. Rules and themes evident before and
explored in previous houses now find more definite expression. All
the individual themes are present, but even more importantly they
are now structured into a significant whole. The design of the
House at Stabio exhibits characteristics that are to become the
well-known traits of Mario Botta's architecture. Its design not only
handles all formal rules with absolute confidence; these rules
become interrelated in such a way as to constitute a unique
identifiable structure. This is a composition of *one*. Everything
comes together; the different aspects of the architectural object
interweave and interrelate. The tower-like house is transformed
into a sign standing in the landscape. Without need for external
references, as it refers only to its own formal structure, it marks a
presence that talks about unity, coherence, and solidity.

Preceding pages: the large opening on the main
facade extends from the roof to the ground level,
revealing its transparency in the nocturnal view

House in Stabio

Facing page: circulation scheme around the central void on the second floor (bedroom zone) and axonometric drawings

Right: detail of the eaves and the skylight on the main facade; detail of the connection of the stairwell column to the roofing, with tapered protrusions of concrete blocks

Chapter Two

Means of Creativity

Banca del Gottardo, Lugano

When compositional logic has reached a level of stability, the transformation of different themes can take place. Transformations on one level generate a series of consequences that upset order on another level and bring into the foreground what was previously hidden. By bringing into prominence what was formerly in the background, or by "making strange" what was familiar and known, transformations of the known and explorations of the unknown become the means of creativity.

The way in which the Ransila Office Building (1981-1985) relates to the corner reveals a deep knowledge of urban morphology and its underlying rules. The elaborate treatment of brick, its protrusions and recesses, also reveals an understanding of the materiality of building and a preference for the expression of the formal by the exploitation of the material. The theme of the wall is pursued. The corporeal nature of architecture is indicated by the shadows of the alternating series of bricks. The field is open for exploration; the brickwork has gained its expressive potential. If in the Chambery Theater and Cultural Center (1982-1987) bricks define the curved surface of the interior, later on, in Mario Botta's churches, they will become a sign of corporeality.

The slight curve on the front facade of the House at Morbio Superiore (1982-1983) brings forward the notion of individualization of the facade. In an undifferentiated universe, one element becomes distinct. The front has been treated as a surface. From now on, formal experimentation is limitless. The front becomes a separate volume, extruding, moving forward in the House at Breganzona (1984-1988). What used to be contained within the limits of the primary solid now becomes the main element. The Banca del Gottardo in Lugano (1982-1988) answers the question of scale by breaking down the volume into four extruding towers, four similar fronts. Frontality is explored further. The Mediatheque in Villeurbanne (1984-1988) faces the street with an enigmatic face. The facade is almost detached from the rest of the building. As if this formal gesture needs to be further signified, end corners become sharp, hide their volumetric solidity and accentuate the two-dimensionality of the surface. The Watari-um Art Gallery in

Tokyo (1985-1990) also takes up the theme. The face becomes a
mask. The facade is no longer only a front; it speaks about the
building itself.

The architecture of Mario Botta is the architecture of mass. The
cylinder holds a special place in his choice of primary solids, its
reading is clear and unambiguous. It is chosen as an autonomous
form, a form that can stand up in an indifferent environment
and give the building presence. In its various appearances, the
continuous curve—the compact, self-enclosed form—consistently
reaffirms its power to be expressive. The ordered subtractions of the
House at Stabio give way to the prominence of the emptied part
defined by the green metal structure at the Residences and Office
Building in Lugano-Paradiso (1986-1992). The same concept, with
its emphasis on the horizontal this time, defines the Home for the
Elderly in Novazzanno (1992-1997). Symbolism and clarity of the
cylindrical form are chosen to represent collective space, be it a
theater or a church. A cylindrical interior surface can be "read" at
once. Space claims its intelligibility. The cylinder can also be
dissected; its half defining the turn of the corner and giving the
street a face at the Union Bank of Switzerland in Basel (1986-
1995). With a sharp difference in scale, it gives form to the House
at Montagnola (1989-1994). Truncated once more, both halved and
elliptical in plan, it creates a powerful atrium for the Harting Office
Building in Minden (1999). Then, once again reduced only to a
retaining wall, the cylinder shapes gallery space in the Friedrich
Dürrenmatt Center, in Neuchâtel (1992-2000).

Ransila Office Building

Lugano, Switzerland, 1981-1985

Corner buildings enjoy a special place in urban typology. A corner is where two different parts of urban structure meet, where different street elevations come together as one. A building placed on a corner used to respond to the situation, take account of it. Has the typology of corner buildings been overlooked by the modern movement? The situation is real and calls for attention.

The Ransila Office Building is a proper corner building. A massive tower is placed at the corner, carrying the weight of the rest of the building. The gradual emptying of the virtual solid, this play with existing and absent mass, with an absence that leaves its imprint on the ordered geometrical articulation of the emptied part, makes this one of the most powerful and distinct articulations of a corner building.

The volume of the building follows rules of elevation set by the two street facades. However, this is a building not only with a corner, but also with a top. The base is emptied out to reveal the shop fronts. The entrance to the office building is placed on the corner; the articulation of the floors is clear and straightforward. Distinguished from the hollowing out of the volume at its base, the top becomes complete again. The perimeter of the boundary, continuous once more, equates with the reading of the virtual volume. A series of round openings at the top, round holes on a closed surface, form a striking contrast with the square openings that articulate the facades in ordered repetition.

The material used is brick: beautifully ordered and elaborate, detailed in protrusions and recesses; it gives a special sense of materiality to the facade. This is not just a cladding. It is not a simple two-dimensional treatment of the vertical plane. Brick becomes a decorative element. It is perhaps the first time that a building by Mario Botta achieves such a distinct materiality. Experiments with the turning at angles of layers of bricks, or, later, of stones, with their shadows and illumination, and experiments

The urban setting seen from the square

Facing page: the corner segment is separated by the geometric variation of the floors

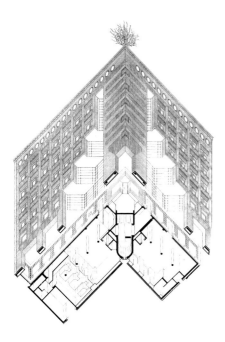

with layering to emphasize the materiality and solidity of the wall, are to constitute, from now on, one of the architect's main themes—the wall. The materiality of the wall is alluring in the formation of mass. The play of shadows in the careful detailing of the facades accentuates thickness. The building's material nature becomes not just a means for the expression of its character, but a powerful sign in itself that speaks about the nature of the making of the artifact, the art of creation.

The highlight in the treatment of the corner is a maple tree planted on the top. Through subtle reference to a tree that grew accidentally on the top of a tower in Lucca, a town in Tuscany, this tree becomes an affirmative statement. What was only insinuated before in the handling of the material, is, now, by the presence of the tree, asserted clearly and explicitly. The tree represents nature, the passing of time, the change of seasons and the relationship of architecture to the sky, not only to the ground. Most of all, it reveals the difference between the natural and the artificial. "A building changes the situation of nature into a situation of culture," Mario Botta says. "What you take from the ground, you can still put on the top," he affirms. The tree, thus, on the top of the corner, becomes the sign that speaks in elegant abstraction for the building itself; for it is a product of man, a product of the artificial. Nature and artifice cannot remain apart. By means of a symbolic gesture, they can be reunited and come together in this impressive corner building.

Facing page: detail of the tree on the corner   Above: axonometric view from below
segment, a sign of changing seasons; below,
the new building seen in the streetfront context

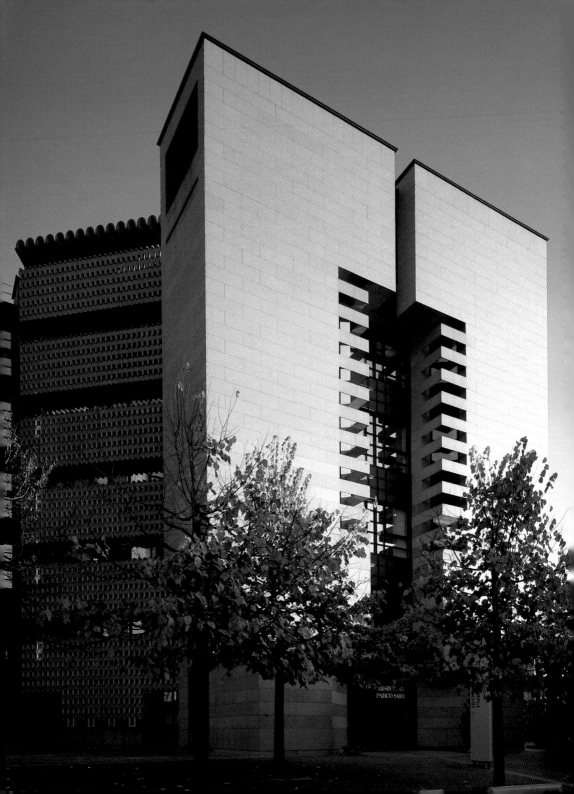

Banca del Gottardo in Lugano

Lugano, Switzerland, 1982-1988

For Mario Botta there is no difference between the small and the large-scale building. Each building has to create a presence in the landscape or the city in which it is built; each building is equally important. The Banca del Gottardo, a prizewinner in an architectural competition, has just such a strong presence. It is on a site adjacent to late nineteenth-century neoclassical villas, on an intersection between the city center and the residential areas of the city suburbs. The site is composed of four typical twentieth-century grid plots, each one of them having been previously occupied by a detached house. The resulting facade, with a continuous elevation of 140 meters, already seemed out of scale in relation to the context. As a result, the architect decided to break the scale by creating four identical units in the form of towers.

Instead of imposing its large mass on the streetfront, the breaking up of the volume plays with the theme of repetition of identical units, succeeding not only in diminishing scale, but also in emphasizing the unique identity of the building. The concept is, more than anything, an urban concept, as it is a response to the singularity of buildings on the street. It marks the end of the urban typology before the residential areas begin.

The building faces the city with a mask, a mask that is multiplied by four. "The facades on the Viale," explains Botta, "are 'complete' images, masks of stone, new faces, urban figures in the context of the city, like the palaces of old. Every building is a part of the city which it is in, something new which enriches the variety and complexity of urban life."[1] This powerful image stands in dialogue with the urban scale, without sacrificing the need to defend its originality and presence. A vertical axis, enlarged at the bottom and tapering towards the top, signifies the entrance. The face remains enigmatic; horizontal slits reveal large glass surfaces at the back. The towers protrude while the rest of the building remains to the rear. Open public spaces, beautifully landscaped in the order of the whole, bring together the public and private realms.

Each tower is marked by a special function on the ground floor: a restaurant, the main banking hall, the entrance for the personnel, and an art gallery. The hexagon used in the Library at the Capuchin Convent reappears in this case to give shape to units which are separated by staircase towers. All four units are connected on the upper floors. Externally aligned offices with a central connecting corridor form the office typology on different floors. A triangular void in the middle of each one of the four units intensifies the clarity of spatial structure. This void, flooded with light by the skylights in the roof, introduces a spatial element for orientation and visual communication. It becomes, as Mario Botta describes it, a "reference marker."

One of the four towers
on Viale Stefano Franscini

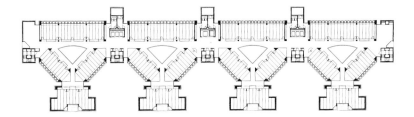

Preceding pages: the urban context;
below, sketch of two towers and
typical floor plan

The rear facade is linear—its linearity broken
only by the protruding staircase-towers. Prefabricated elements alternating with stone create a
kind of *brise-soleil* for the facade, a theme that
also gives the setback parts of the front facade a
delicate texture. The vertical and the horizontal
interweave to form a mature composition. The
verticality of the towers at the front becomes the
means by which the strong identity of the
building is asserted. The emphasis on the
horizontal throughout the rest of the building
introduces an element of antithesis in the
composition. Texture also plays the same formal
game. Smooth pink and grey granite cladding for
the towers alternates with textured 'brise-soleil'
on the rest of the building. Horizontal, two-tone
lines mark the base of the towers. Cladding
motifs, on the other hand, overlap with the
formal theme of "emptying out the volume."
Each class of formal rules for the volume and the
surface or the materials emphasizes one aspect; all
of them, in close interrelation, interweave into
what becomes a powerful composition. Small
variations on the themes, on the other hand, are
always present in order to create variety, tension,
or deviations from the rule, to create diversity
and, thus, to make the sign direct, yet intriguing.

Detail of the lower part of one of the towers,
with the bank entrance

Facing page: the sequence of the four towers
and courtyards

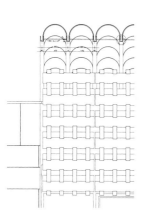

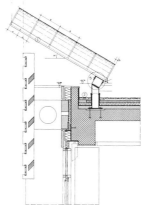

Detail of the sunscreen elements in concrete
and stone slabs attached to the structure in
front of the large facade glazing

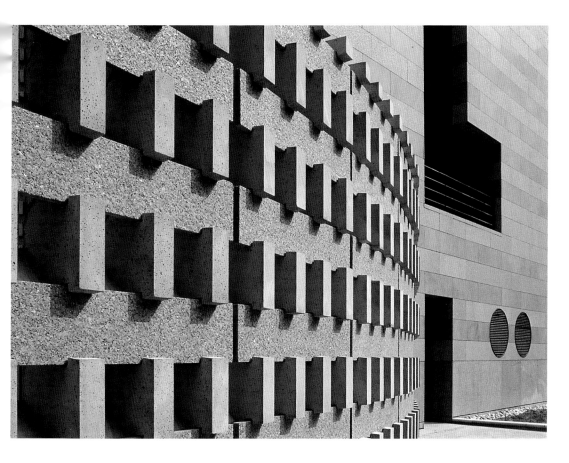

Facade effect of the sunscreen elements

Access to the interior space of the hall of the
bank with the client zone

House in Morbio Superiore

Morbio Superiore, Ticino, Switzerland, 1982-1983

Placed on a hilly site, with its volume almost square, the house in Morbio Superiore regards the world with an enigmatic face. Mario Botta recalls: "…I wanted to hollow out the form inside and cut the house out of the hill with a knife so to speak, using only the floor at the top as the entrance. The slightly curved facade, on the other hand, belongs more to the landscape than to the house itself. For this reason, it is a concave facade which taps light and makes it resonate at different times of the day… the house in Morbio has something of a cave, while at the same time it opens out to the sky. Although you remain in your home, you retain some relationship to the outside world."[2]

The architect chooses to single out the front facade and to individualize it. It is not a matter, however, of only distinct treatment in relation to one side of the primary solid, as in the previous houses. The facade, in this case, is also treated as a surface. The rule of frontality –the way the house faces the world– is brought to the foreground. The southern facade, in dialogue with the view, becomes slightly curved. Right in the middle, on its axis of symmetry, a deep covered terrace combines the horizontal orthogonal of the negative space with the vertical element of the deep incision and the skylight. The horizontality of the facade and the terrace, and the emphasis placed on the vertical by the accentuation of the axis, create a composition where antithetical elements are integrated into a whole. The powerful ordering of the mass needs to be supplemented by more subtle gestures; the surface of the slightly curving inflection of the facade is highlighted by a series of alternating plain and silver-painted concrete blocks laid out straight and set at an angle of forty-five degrees. The front of the building remains the external surface of a volume, suspended between autonomy and subversion, between the dialectics of surface and mass. On the face of the building, mass and plane, geometrical order, texture, light, and shadow interweave in elegant architectural play.

Although the way the house faces the world, its internal organization and spatial structure are ruled by symmetry, entry is, as always, from the side. The corner is emptied out and the wall becomes curved. The large portico mediates between the external world and the protected world inside. Having entered from the top, one descends to the other two floors that are partly hidden in the ground. Light pours in through the skylight. The vertical axis emphasized by the skylight on top and the alternating series of

concrete slabs initiate play between light—the luminosity of the wall—and shadow—the transparency of the roof and the shadows of the deep cuts. Nothing extrudes; everything is contained.

While in the previous houses by Mario Botta it was important to deal with overall order and the setting up of rules, now, in this House, transformations in the mass, the texture and the treatment of the exterior are accepted. Having mastered the order of rules, composition can now allow for deviations. The rules that bring everything together, however, that make the house a sign of *one*, a sign of an autonomous, self-contained object, where every aspect intensifies its reading, are not broken. Instead, they find a new expression.

The extraordinary position of the house on the hill

Interior spaces organized around the terrace

André Malraux
Theater and Cultural Center

Chambéry, France, 1982-1987

An enormous square building with a courtyard in the middle, the Napoleonic barracks dominated a large area of open ground surrounded by a tight urban fabric of nineteenth-century buildings. The contrast in scale was provocative; the site presented a real challenge. However, the competition brief for the Andre Malraux Cultural Center asked only for the restoration of the barracks and the design of a 900-seat multi-purpose hall. For Mario Botta this was a chance to redefine the relationships between existing and new buildings, to reconstruct part of the urban fabric on the outskirts of a historic city. For him: "Architects today find themselves at a fork in the road: they must either continue to support the current attitude of destroying the structure of urban forms, or attempt through the proposal of alternatives to reposition the city (understood as a formal expression of history) at the center of interest for any architectural undertaking. These days, the choice is to build for the city or build against the city."[3]

The theater building is placed off the axis of symmetry in the old building, keeping parallel to the street line. Connected to the barracks by a glass-enclosed bridge, it is actually entered from the courtyard. Its volumetric composition consists of two major volumes, a half cylinder that forms the theater hall, and an orthogonal one that forms the stage. The long linear volume of an open emergency stair protrudes perpendicular to the street. The linearity of the staircase contrasts with the cylindrical mass and defines the limits of the plaza formed by the theater, the barracks, and a previously-existing building. The theater hall, almost circular in shape, is surrounded by a three-story-high perimeter, which houses access routes and stairs. The cylinder is emptied out at the ground level to reveal a series of round columns marking the entrance to the foyer placed on the perimeter. The mass is becoming complete with the upper part, restoring the reading of the solid volume.

The building is clad in alternating horizontal zones of stone and concrete. The zigzagged treatment of the surface in the curved interior of the theater hall, first used by Mario Botta in the House at Morbio Superiore, gives the interior a unique materiality. Thus, a theme explored in one project reappears in another. The interior surface gains volumetric qualities. Light and shadow, acoustic properties and texture come together, closely interwoven into one.

Mario Botta's use of the cylinder is usually to signify a building that stands autonomously within its surroundings. In the Chambéry Theater, however, the architect's preference for a round shape for the collective space, for the theater hall, dictates his choice. If shapes have any meaning, then the round one talks about the feeling of collectivity. However, the cylinder, even though prominent, does not stand in isolation. This is a composition of two major elements. The rectangle of the stage also has a role to play, as

Facing page: detail of the emergency
staircases inside the structure of a flying arch

View of the theater from the east

its linear sides are parallel to the street line. The bringing together of the two volumes along the axis of symmetry creates a virtual axis, which, even if it is implied, manages to create a strong sense of directionality. The mass of the building stands both in juxtaposition and in relation to the barracks. The distinction between rectilinear and cylindrical forms, the breaking up of the rectilinear part into a composition of volumes as well as the subtle relation in their proportions, contributes to the formal quality. This is a project that aims to restore urbanity. A strong new presence is introduced to counterbalance the enormous scale of the barracks. Tension created between the two masses is a conscious choice.

The building is composed of the taller volume of the stage area and the lower volume of the semicircular seating area, placed against the existing barracks

Detail of the walls in concrete alternated with stone slabs containing the external staircases

Facing page: first floor corridor

Preceding pages: the staircase connects the
two corridors around the large hall and the
internal space of the foyer

The large hall of the theater
Right: perspective section

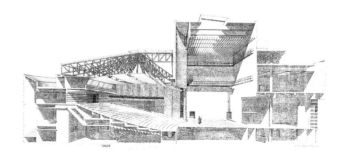

House in Breganzona

Breganzona, Ticino, Switzerland, 1984-1988

Standing on the corner of two roads, in a hilly area near Lugano, this private house in Breganzona extends, like other houses by Mario Botta, to three floors. The entrance is on the ground floor, together with an office and space for services. The day area is placed on the first floor, while the night zone is on the third. This is more of an L-shaped plan inscribed within a square envelope. The various uses, allocated to different floors, follow the overall geometrical order of the plan. It is only on the third floor that the interior extends to the limits of the square, and integrates the shape of the volume. The staircase, placed in the corner, creates balance within an interior void that links the three levels of the house visually. Emphasis is on the diagonal; this diagonal, however, actually remains defined only by the outside space. A series of terraces creates a "microclimate," which allows for continuity of the interior, spreading out to the exterior. The house is constructed using cement blocks, which alternate on the exterior wall with horizontal strips of silicon-glazed cement blocks. The expressiveness of the material which is used in the House at Morbio Superiore to place emphasis on the front facade, in this case, takes over the whole surface.

This house marks a turning point, as the primary solid of previous houses by Mario Botta has now given way to a more complex volumetric composition. An orthogonal volume has been inserted diagonally into the square block. This volume presents a powerful front, emphasized as it is by the vertical surfaces of its two endings, as well as the twin cylindrical skylights. Semi-open spaces are created on different levels: a grand covered portico on the second floor; a belvedere on the top. The notion of transitional space—of the space that mediates between the inside and the

outside—which was originally created by means of successive subtractions from the primary volume in other houses, now becomes an independent formal element. It is not just a negative space shaped by the hollowing out of the volume; it moves to the foreground and gains autonomous presence. The theme of frontality becomes primary. Transformations in the synthesis of the volume create a powerful front.

Composition does not emphasize the presence of the primary solid any longer. The two interpenetrating volumes do not express only solidity and mass. Tension is created with the introduction of the directional force of the new element. In its forward projection it carries with it the surface on the upper part of the square volume: walls are curved, projected outside the perimeter, attempting to follow the vertical element in its movement to the front. Form becomes more complex.

The site near Lugano; the house is oriented toward the southwest

Facade detail with the curved wall of the second floor that extends to wrap around the entrance portico

Detail of the transparent structure covering
the external volume

The main facade follows the diagonal axis
of the house

Facing page: the space of the external loggia

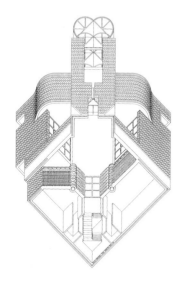

What was previously part of the formal manipulation of the primary solid is now transformed into a unique element that expresses the relationship of the inside to the outside, the way the building faces the world. Form becomes expressive. An underlying notion of forward movement upsets the formation of the mass. A notion potent in its spatiality becomes transformed into an architectural feature with great expressive power.

Facing page: the stairwell, a structure in iron and wood, is lit by a rooftop skylight

Axonometric drawings from below and from above

Interior of the living room

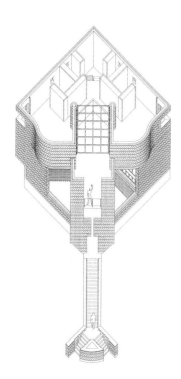

Mediatheque

Villeurbanne, France, 1984-1988

Set within the continuous facade of Emile Zola Avenue, the building responds to its neighbors with a subtle gesture: the front moves forward to become aligned with the building to the right, while the other part goes back to align with the building to the left. In this way, it takes into account the two street lines: the original building line of the nineteenth century and the setback line which was established after the Second World War, when it was assumed that old buildings would be demolished and the street widened. The orthogonal volume that makes the junction is clad in glass blocks, while the protruding front and the semicircular back are clad in alternating strips of beige and dark gray stone. An impressive opening on the stone front intensifies the vertical axis and gives light to the entrance lobby, while the blank walls hide staircases in their sharp corners. The Mediatheque space is allocated two volumes, one orthogonal and the other semi-cylindrical, the two brought together by an impressive cylindrical atrium that penetrates the whole and floods the interior with light.

The atrium becomes the heart of the composition: "The idea from the outset was to construct a central element of reference. And this corresponds to the necessity I feel to find a 'backbone' in every project, so that people entering the building will have a chance to orient themselves. It could be a shaft of light

or a structural element. The idea for the competition was to make a house made of empty space within the solid building, with connecting stairs winding around the void…This space was born more of an intuition of light…".[4]

The originality of a front broken in volume by four towers in the Banca del Gottardo is transformed in the Mediatheque into a powerful element. This building has a definite front, which moves forward and thus becomes dissected from the main volume. Its sharp edges create the illusion of a plane. The twin parts, created by the vertical cut in the middle, break down its length. Verticality needs to be reinstated; it asserts the monumentality of the facade.

The front becomes a face, a plane dressed in alternating strips of stone. The cylinder, also clad in strips of stone, follows the rule. The two protruding elements are different from the orthogonal volume in glass blocks. Distinctions between materials, between the solid and the transparent, accentuate the volumetric composition.

The apparent clarity of geometry does not hide the underlying complexity of the gestures employed. The creation of a face for the building, or the tectonic quality of the atrium exhibits a richness that becomes even more significant considering how powerful and direct the message is. Moving from the front to the back, successive symmetrical ordering of the plan generates anticipation of the main event;

Facade on Avenue Emile Zola   Main facade with slender two-tone bands of
                                               stone and large axial incision

an interplay between compact and indefinite space, between the configuration of the exact and the expansiveness of the boundary. This calmly terminates at the focal point, the atrium, while the reading rooms form a perimeter. On the vertical dimension, the atrium becomes increasingly smaller. The concentric cylindrical walls accentuate the verticality of the void space. The visual field is focused and directed to the top, while the gaze is released to experience the richness of space and light.

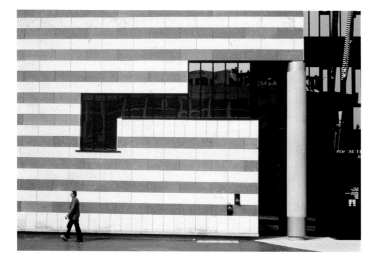

Detail of glazed facade opening

Interior of the young people's library

Next page: entrance level plan and the large central void providing lighting for the interiors

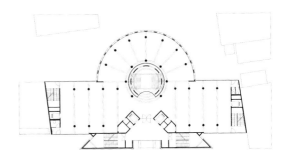

Watari-um Art Gallery

Tokyo, Japan, 1985-1990

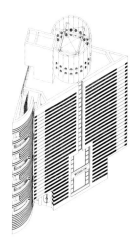

The high cost of land may have made Tokyo a metropolis known for the ephemeral character of its buildings. The Watari-um Art Gallery by Mario Botta is, however, anything but ephemeral. It is, instead, a building of permanence, not only because of the stability with which it stands, the solidity of its stone cladding, and the sobriety of its facades. Permanence is a matter of composition which, by acknowledging the urban situation, creates a building which is transformed into a sign of its own order. In a letter to the owner, Mario Botta writes: "In the Babel of urban languages that changes daily, I wanted to test the 'durability' of a strong, primary image, an architecture generated by the building's own inner logic."[5]

Placed on a triangular site at the intersection of a major thoroughfare and a secondary street, the building takes on the shape of the site and transforms it into a triangular volume. The external boundary is wrapped around an open staircase on the corner, while the technical floor on the roof is transformed into a special formal element: a cylinder that crowns the top. The building houses a bookshop on the basement and ground-floor levels, exhibition rooms on the first, second, and third floors, while the top floor accommodates offices and the residence of the owner. It is a concrete structure; external walls are clad with prefabricated concrete panels alternating with black granite, while the inside ones consist of white cement bricks.

Frontality and accentuation of the corner, two gestures that acknowledge the urban condition, become the primary features of the project. Urbanity is once more the starting point. The form follows, takes the initiative and transforms the given situation. The corner staircase distances itself from the front facade by the curvature of its surface. The gesture is subtle. The front wall needs to regain its autonomy. A long incision cuts vertically into the facade and opens up into a large window front. This is a building of surfaces. There is no emptying out of the volume to reveal its solidity. The solid is expressed only by means of the two-dimensional boundary. Mass is hidden behind the expressive power of the wall.

The building faces the world with a mask. The theme, explored at the Banca del Gottardo and the Mediatheque at Villeurbanne, reappears. The facade becomes even more autonomous. The vertical plane is almost detached from the volume. The front does not disclose the actual number of floors. What is behind the facade is covered by the alternating rhythm of horizontal strips of cladding. One needs to enter the building to discover what it was made for. This is a theme Mario Botta introduces

Main facade on the street, accented by the volume of the external staircase at the corner; axonometric

later on in his museums; the building stands silent on the street, without revealing its internal organization. The large surfaces needed for exhibition purposes in the interior become a requirement resolved by formal elaboration. The challenge of the primary volume standing intact, of the front facade becoming a mask, of the surface being a sign without the intrusion of obligatory openings to the outside world, is taken up. The provocative power of the silent stone wall supercedes the ephemeral character of the architecture of the city; it creates a sign of an archetypal architecture that extends beyond the limits of time.

The chaotic urban context;   Facing page: detail of the hollowed corner
interior of the gallery on the second floor

Union Bank of Switzerland

Basel, Switzerland, 1986-1995

Although this is a corner site between two roads, as in the case of the Ransila Office Building, the Headquarters of the Union Bank of Switzerland negates the theme employed for that corner building. The competition brief asked for the design of an end building, a corner building on a nineteenth-century boulevard, opposite the entrance to the old city of Basel. What seemed more important for the architect, however, was to create a face for it on the main road in order to consolidate its presence in relation to the station. "It seemed," Mario Botta recalls, "more important to bring the main road to a logical and convincing architectural conclusion before it turned the corner to encounter the more open twentieth-century construction along the road running perpendicular to it. So the project developed from an urban rather than an architectural reading of the situation... So once again typological choices were determined by the morphological tensions of the surrounding city."[5]

The building is composed of a semi-cylinder clad in stone with horizontal strips that alternate in color. The cylinder is linked to a small villa, which houses the restaurant. The turning point on the corner connects two parts of the city, which poses an interesting problem. The continuity of the building blocks on the one side contrasts with the discontinuity of separate houses on the other. In order to connect the two contrasting parts, Mario Botta cuts half of the cylindrical volume. What is then presented as a massive cylinder on one side, firmly touching on the ground, is transformed into a sharp plane on the other. One has only to turn the corner to see how abruptly the cylindrical form is cut to reveal a vertical surface, which is accentuated even further by vertical slits as well as by the treatment of the stone cladding. On this side, the building can now respond to the individual houses.

The ground floor, planned initially for commercial use, and later on as an exhibition gallery, houses the banking hall. The other floors are allocated for office use. The entrance is organized on the ground floor on the axis of symmetry. An atrium, illuminated by a skylight, brings light to the interior, and organizes the distribution of corridors on different floors. Successive floors are recessed in the back street, in order to follow height regulations. The atrium also becomes smaller at the top; this gradual tapering in size is an elegant morphological feature of the building. A kind of symmetrical scale interrupts the stone-clad wall with a series of vertical windows revealing large glass surfaces at the back. Windows, forming vertical and round cuts on the wall in rhythmical repetition, alternate with glass surfaces in dark aluminum frames; features of the formal vocabulary of the architect are used to create a strong identifiable image for the building.

As in the case of the Casa Rotonda in Stabio, the use of the cylinder does not hinder Mario Botta from resolving the issue of implied directionality of form by carefully carving the volume in order to create a strong vertical axis on what could be defined as the "front" of the cylinder. On the contrary, having previously resolved the issue of how the undifferentiated round surface of a cylinder can be transformed

The corner of the building with its vertical
surface accentuated by two openings

The curved facade of the building on the Aeschenplatz

Plans of the ground floor and the top floor

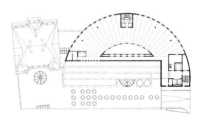

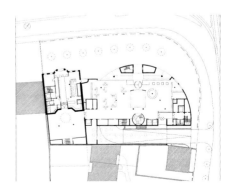

to a front, the cylindrical form is now chosen, not only to integrate the corner into a volume, but precisely in order to present a front to the street. While in the Watari-um Gallery, the front distinguishes itself as a two-dimensional plane, and the turn of the corner is resolved by the sharp angle of the open staircase, in this case, the concave surface of the cylinder solves both the issue of frontality and the street corner. The issue is taken up by the volume, a distinctive treatment allowing the cylinder to give the street corner an identifiable conclusion, creating an urban front.

Detail of the recessing of the curved facade
and the connection to the existing villa

Facing page: the large central space
overlooked by the offices (with an artwork by
Felice Varini)

Centro Cinque Continenti
Offices and Residences

Lugano-Paradiso, Switzerland, 1986-1992

Placed near the lake of Lugano, the Centro Cinque Continenti is a strong presence in this part of the city. Oriented toward the lake, it breaks from the typical orientation of other buildings in the area. "I wondered," Mario Botta recalls, "if instead of putting a building in the city, it mightn't be possible to put the city in the building, so I tried swapping everything around. Instead of a 'solid' I designed a 'void' so that the image of the city could be incorporated in the building as a backdrop. The brick perimeter wall forms an outer shell, which encloses the functional space within, while also delineating a square central court. The result is a house within a house, ennobled with glass blocks to identify the public domain of the circulation areas."[7]

The cylindrical volume of the building, which is clad in brick, is generously hollowed out to form a large semi-interior courtyard covered by a glass and metal roof. The ground floor is allocated for commercial use, while the next three floors house offices. Three more floors with apartments are placed above the glass and metal roof, with their terraces open to views of the lake and the mountains.

The primary form of the cylinder is used once more by Mario Botta to create an autonomous object, which is a microcosm in itself; an object with strong permanence that can withstand an indifferent environment. At the same time, the usual emptying out of the volume, so characteristic of his giving of form, moves to the foreground this time, creating an independent existence. It becomes larger than usual. It acquires a top in the form of a slightly curved, transparent, glass and metal roof. It also acquires walls, in a glass block and metal structural framework, formed by the circulation corridors of the office floors. A veritable glass house is formed inside the courtyard, a new formal element that differentiates itself from the rest of the building. Its transparency accentuates the solidity of the cylindrical volume. The brick cladding is treated with delicate horizontal zoning, while the alternating rhythm of windows, vertical slits for the offices, square or round for the apartments, appears as a series of holes on the brick surface. The light green of the metal structure, intensifying the distinction between the two entities, accentuates the warm color of the brick.

If the cylinder has, by definition, no orientation, the large opening gives the volume a definite orientation. By further exploring the potential of the primary form, the architect experiments with void, with negative space. The building does not simply address the external world with a face; instead, it creates a courtyard which invites the external world, thus including it within the

The building oriented with the opening of the courtyard in the direction of the lake; the nocturnal view reveals the transparency of the 'skin' in iron and glass bricks inside the courtyard.

Detail of the reticular structure over the internal
courtyard

View toward the lake from the landing of the
staircase on the upper level

The site seen from the lake

Axonometric

Facing page: the structure in iron and glass
bricks encloses the internal circulation system
for the offices and apartments

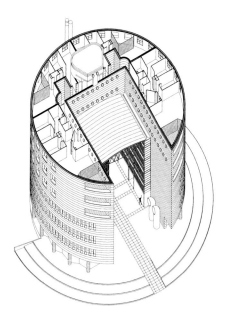

boundary of its presence. It is, indeed, a very subtle way in which Mario Botta introduces a variation on his theme. The void becomes larger. It is treated as an autonomous element in the composition, using different materials and color. The void is no longer just the intermediate space between the inside and the outside; it is a new element. By bringing the city into the building, the architect also enriches his vocabulary. Through its dialogue with the surroundings, the Centro Cinque Continenti introduces an interesting departure from the typology of round buildings that Botta has designed thus far. Without forfeiting its autonomy, the building restates its wish to initiate a dialogue with the city.

House in Montagnola

Montagnola, Ticino, Switzerland, 1989-1993

Standing on a serene landscape overlooking a lake, the house is a half-cylinder intersected by a low rectilinear volume. This volume houses the swimming pool and the sauna, and is connected to another rectangle for the owner's collection of cars. The house comprises three floors. The entrance is on the middle floor, with access from the terrace created on top of the rectilinear volume. The nighttime zone occupies the ground and first floors, while the second floor is allocated to daytime activities. A large hollowing out of the volume at the front creates terraces, intermediate spaces between inside and outside. As in other houses by Mario Botta, the structure is in concrete, with double walls and brick cladding.

What appears as a cylinder in the front part is revealed as a sharp plane at the back. The surprising effect of the cut cylinder of the Union Bank of Switzerland that created a front for the street now reappears, scaled down. Formal transformations cut across the matter of scale. A theme can always be reinvented in the light of a different situation.

The volume has a back and a front. It is no longer a cylinder, an autonomous object standing in the landscape like the House in Stabio. By cutting the volume in half, the house gains definite directionality. Its front, the cylindrical part, opens to the view with large glass surfaces. Subtractions from the primary volume create terraces. Once more, the volume becomes complete at the top so that the reading of the primary solid is clear. Circular openings emphasize the front facade. The back facade, on the other hand, remains shielded, perforated only by the glass rectangle created by the skylight.

As in his other houses, Mario Botta chooses to relate to the view with careful elaboration of the front. This front, however, no longer has an axis of symmetry intensified by the emptying out of the volume and the skylight on the roof. There is no axiality in the composition of the volume, or in the organization of the inside. The internal void that visually connects all floors in Mario Botta's houses is now placed at the back. All elements do not aim at

View of the long terrace joining the indoor pool
to the house proper

Interior view of the pool facing the garden;
right, the stairwell

View of the western facade with the large lawn

Facing page: axonometric and the rear facade
of the house, facing the street

intensifying the main theme, that of a primary object, standing out
distinctly in the landscape. In a departure from his other houses,
this is a composition of two volumes. The volumetric
experimentation upsets order and introduces interesting variations
on the themes.

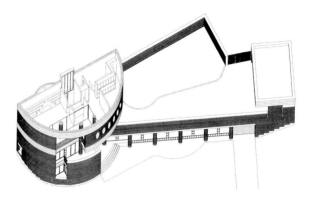

Home for the Elderly

Novazzano, Italy, 1992-1997

A building is a complex organization. Walls border and differentiate space, create subdivisions, rooms, and circulation areas. To know where you are, to find your way through and be able to read the spatial structure, or have what is referred to as "spatial intelligibility," is an important property in a building, even more so if this is a home for the elderly. A building of this kind needs clear spatial organization and a point of reference. This point of reference, a place in double height for group activities, and a magnificent portico that opens to the view, become the central concept in the design of the Home for the Elderly in Novazzano.

On a slight slope, overlooking the urbanized landscape of the Mendrisiotto plain, the building takes the form of a low cylinder elegantly clad in brick. Part of the cylinder is missing, revealing a grand opening to the view, creating the transitional space that is to be found in most buildings by Mario Botta. Like a grand hotel placed in a garden, the building is entered from the back, and opens up to the view through the articulation of its front. A notional axis penetrates the transparent core of the building and opens to a perspective of the view.

There are two more floors, apart from the ground floor that is the public part. The common spaces and the multipurpose hall of double height provide a place of interest and a focus for guests as well as giving the building a definite core. Centrality becomes a main theme. Twenty-five rooms, with small, protected terraces, are placed on the perimeter on each level, while circulation winds around the core.

As in many other cases, the cylinder is chosen as a distinct form, as a primary solid. The volume accepts formal articulation. Parts are subtracted. Negative space, the missing part, is as ordered as what remains; a perfectly symmetrical void, crowned by a transparent roof. Continuity of the edges of the boundary is interrupted. The scale of the missing part does not allow for the completion of the volume. As if the void has gained an existence of its own, the negative volume penetrates into the real one. Subtraction emphasizes the solidity of the volume, creates a front, and brings the inside close to the outside. Instead of the building expanding to include parts of the external world, the external world becomes part of the building itself. The front is not an articulation of the surface, of the facade. It is, instead, an articulation of the volume. Symmetry of the front facade, the play between the horizontal and the vertical, the elaboration of a base, a middle and a skyline, create a designed object that stands calmly on the site.

Its geometry brings to mind the Centro Cinque Continenti. The generous emptying out of the central core of a cylinder to create an inner courtyard reappears. This time, however, the skyline of the building does not oppose the line of the earth; this is a building that extends on the horizontal, not a tower. The unique character of the shape does not speak of independence and autonomy, but aims, in a calm "tone of voice," to create a point of reference in relation to the landscape. The surfaces of the walls set at a forty-five-degree angle, the recessed volumes, the circular column in the middle, the twin

Overall view of the building

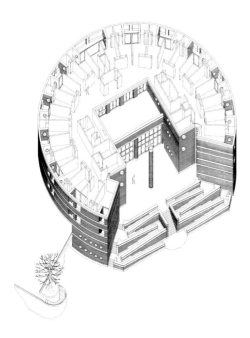

The cylindrical volume with the horizontal
incision of the accessway; axonometric
drawing

cylindrical form of the skylight, and then the cadence of the
leisurely sloping lines of the ramp create a self-contained building—
still a microcosm not in isolation, but in dialogue with the
landscape.

The large two-story community space on
the ground floor with access to the terrace
and the garden

On the following pages: front view with
the recessed roofed terraces overlooking
the garden

Friedrich Dürrenmatt Center

Neuchâtel, Switzerland, 1992-2000

In 1993-1994, when Mario Botta designed the exhibition of Dürrenmatt's graphic works at the Kunsthaus in Zurich, he created a "dark" space bound by black curved walls and a black floor for the drawings and engravings, and a "bright" white space, open, with broad windows for the color paintings. The difference between the two spaces was marked. When asked to design the Dürrenmatt Center, the curved wall reappeared giving shape to the whole building, the contradiction between light and shadow taken up by a tower of light and an underground excavation.

Located in Neuchâtel, a city near the French border, the small museum houses the collection of drawings of the famous Swiss novelist and playwriter Friedrich Dürrenmatt. After his death in 1990, Dürrenmatt's wife decided to show the public these very expressive drawings that were kept private until his death. It was a difficult task to design for the writer and the man, to express the values of an exceptional and unique personality and to give form to his spirit. The first, immediate decision of Mario Botta was to place the building next to Dürrenmatt's home. The idea of architecture direct in its simplicity and dense in its symbolism was to follow.

Placed on a hilly site, the museum is defined by a heavy round wall and a tower. The wall creates a kind of a platform, an open terrace for an appreciation of the view. Exhibits are hidden underneath in the double-height exhibition galleries. Placed next to the existing house that houses Dürrenmatt's library and a small cafeteria, the museum is signalled by an access tower illuminated brightly by skylights from above. This stone-clad tower placed on the axis of symmetry of the wall creates a point of reference for the underground building.

The visitor approaches from the back. Entering through a small lobby between the house and the tower, the visitor enters on a kind of bridge that forms an implied axis inside the tower, an axis also indicated by the glass surface on one side and the round glass on the other side of the walls. Led via a spacious staircase to the mezzanine floor where a small projection room and hall are located, the visitor then moves down to the main floor. Light from above illuminates the curved wall that borders the exhibition spaces. Concrete construction with gray slate cladding 10 cm thick contributes to the massiveness of the walls on the exterior; gray slate is also used for the floors.

An introverted space, a space for contemplation and appreciation of the collection, this building

The large exhibition hall features perimeter skylights. Right: facade of the volume above ground clad in black slate blocks

shapes and is shaped by the site. The gradual lowering of slopes that point to the gate at the center of the round walls, and the verticality of the tower which matches the neighboring house in height, are elements on the axis of symmetry of the whole, leading to the platform. The building does not disclose its mass. Its facade becomes a retaining wall; it has no openings. The introverted space inside needs no interference from the outside.

The museum is actually hidden. The tower of light and the retaining wall are the only references to its existence; the vertical and the horizontal start a dialogue with the landscape. What becomes important is the process of entering, of moving from the outside to the inside, of moving down to the lower part where the precious drawings are kept. The underground building strongly parallels the nature of the exhibits. Descending into a world of art, descending to where the private is exposed to the public is a ceremonial procedure. Anticipation is heightened; order controls haste. Gradually revealed to eager eyes, space does not need a reference point to be read. It is there—self-contained, serene, evocative. Clear lines and volumes—an architecture of the new gently takes care of the old, where the writer lived and left his traces as it stands protectively next to its memories. It is an architecture of the primordial in a dialogue with the landscape, its light, and its essence. When the new meets the old, their coming together has the fragility of a precious encounter, and the penetrating and decisive nature of what has already belonged.

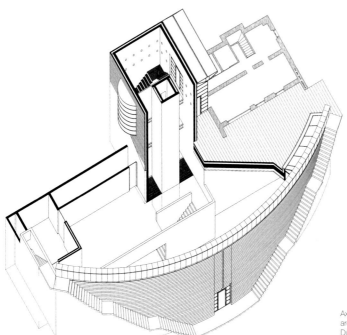

Axonometric. Facing page: view of the large arched hall. The painting is by Friedrich Dürrenmatt, entitled "The last general assembly of the National Banking Institute"

Tower entrance with stairwell. Facing page:
above, preliminary sketch by Mario Botta;
below, the roofing of the underground space
forms a large terrace at ground level

Chapter Three

Form and Meaning

Cymbalista Synagogue and Jewish Heritage Centre

Form does not need to rely on external references in order to be meaningful: it does not necessarily need to be referential to have meaning. Its constitution offers a basis on which signification can rest. Mario Botta's architecture is, indeed, rich in potential for meaning. Underlying his design there is a strong structure that regulates the generation of space and form. When, however, form and space also need to speak about something else, Mario Botta's architecture becomes almost symbolic. This is the case with his churches. In coming to terms with the house of God, the expressive potential of his form-giving explodes.

The symbolic gesture of upward movement in a church becomes transformed into the truncated cylinder of the Church in Mogno (1986/92-1998). Use of material is poetic. Alternating series of stones create illusions. Floor and wall unite and, in their massiveness, contradict the transparency of the roof: structure and material, geometry and form, axes of symmetry order the whole. The emptying out of mass shapes the wall so that the gaze is guided towards the vastness of sky. The truncated cylinder also gives form to the Cathedral in Evry (1988-1995). The double wall and the elaboration of the roof explore the difference in scale. Nature and the passing of time are addressed by the presence of trees that crown the top. The theme, introduced in the Ransila Office Building, reappears, full of symbolism. On the other hand, the linear bridge and its cylindrical base in the Chapel of Santa Maria degli Angeli (1990-1996) give interpretation to the site and the vastness of the view. Movement towards the infinite, seclusion and introspection, the celebration of the mountains and the spiritual, and the awe of the breathtaking view combined with the meditative power of the dark walls, condense meaning.

The two cylinders used in the Cymbalista Synagogue and Jewish Heritage Centre (1997-1998) emphatically announce the double nature of the space. Form cannot be confined only to referring to its constitution any longer. Its expressive potential exceeds these limits. The truncated cylinder is multiplied. Form is not afraid of being inspired by nature. Like a stone cloverleaf, the Church at Malpensa Airport (1998) raises its three cylinders to the sky.

Its referentiality relies on the essential. Form-giving elevates the essence of space. However, symbolism is never direct, for expressiveness of form is only a means. Even when it becomes almost anthropomorphic, as in the Cumbre de las Americas Monument in Santa Cruz de la Sierra, Bolivia (1996), it is still based on formal order and the reading of the site.

Mario Botta says that the museum is the modern Cathedral. The San Francisco Museum of Modern Art (1989-1995) might not be like the Evry Cathedral; its form, perhaps, is not such a powerful single gesture. It cannot be, for this is a different kind of building. However, in the way it silently faces the street, in the way it stands up against the skyscrapers in the background, addressing their verticality with its horizontal lines, its truncated cylinder, and its clear spatial structure, it is not far from the symbolism of a building used for worship.

Context can influence form. If frontality is the means by which the building formally responds to the context, it is only one step away from a powerful and intriguing context that will also shape the building. The Jean Tinguely Museum (1993-1997) is shaped by its context. Its structure, its elevations, its "barca," the bridge-like-corridor as a metaphor of a boat, respond to this context. The autonomous building of the early years gives way to interplay with the site. Form is no less self-contained. However, in its dialogue with the context another parameter is introduced. Not everything is interrelated to a higher order by the structure that keeps the whole together. Parts of it can relate to something external. Or, pairs of notions can be in contrast, as in the case of the Municipal Library in Dortmund (1995-1999). The glass cone stands distinct from the linear stone-clad volume, its transparency different from the solidity of the wall, its place at the front distinct from the definition of the linear limit at the rear. And then, form and space can also be "spoken" by another medium. A church, by Borromini, in Rome, becomes transformed by the language of representation, while its Wooden Model in Lugano (1999) stands in suspension between the real and its discourse. Transformations can take place by the *foregrounding*[1] of an element in the composition. Order might be upset, but meaning becomes focused. Form, resting securely on a long-acquired compositional structure, can continuously experiment by exploring the limits between the abstract and the literal, for this is the nature of inspiration and of the poetics of form.

Church of San Giovanni Battista

Mogno, Ticino, Switzerland, 1986/92-1998

Placed at the end of a little village in the Alps, in the upper Val Maggia region, the church is built on the site of the ruins of the seventeenth century church, dedicated to Saint John the Baptist, which was destroyed by an avalanche. "The determination to resist the mountain, to bear witness to something greater than one's own life, the need to consolidate the patrimony of work, the need to overcome the sense of loneliness, the necessity of affirming the hopes and expectations of our time, the need to take action in the space between the absent immensity of the infinite and the consciousness of one's own limits"[2] reveal, in the architect's words, the motives behind the design.

The geometry is simple yet rich and complex at the same time. The volume of the church is a cylinder, elliptical in plan, truncated at the roof in such a way as to make this all-glass roof a perfect circle. According to Rudolph Arnheim[3], circle and ellipsis confront each other in a contrapuntal rhythm. Straight lines, on the other hand, bind the interior. It is an orthogonal space in the floorplan that gradually changes on the vertical dimension to the round shape of the roof, created as if by a design gesture of "subtraction of mass from a primary solid in order to create a void." The massive stone wall, austere in its simplicity on the outside, becomes, through an elegant play of transformations, an expressive element on the interior. Stone gives shape to the geometrical formation of mass. The wall is not just a surface; it has mass. The old-fashioned way of building in the local area, using wide stone blocks, placed on either side, while concrete is poured in, is transformed to a celebration of the concave aspect of the building.

Subtle compositional gestures enrich the potential for signification. The inscription of the rectangle delineates the interior of the church as a place for gathering. This is a rectangle that has its long axis perpendicular to the axis defined by the entrance and the sanctuary—the axis that traditionally constitutes the main procedural axis in a church. Space as a gathering place is differentiated three-dimensionally from the overall volume of the church. From one point onwards, subtraction of mass takes place in such a way as to unite the orthogonal perimeter of the rectangle to the circular shape of the transparent roof. Natural light floods the interior. There are no other perforations on the solid boundary; the volume remains intact. The truncated section, this upward movement of the volume, the symbolic element of the church, becomes integrated with the notion of natural light. Contact with nature, in an idealistic form, becomes direct.

Play with three axes of symmetry enriches the formal order. The entrance and sanctuary define two points of an axis that also has to do with the placement of the church in the landscape. Small recesses in the solid boundary intensify the long axis of symmetry of the rectangle. The truncated section and the strong presence of a double arch on the interior create a third axis. This is a notional axis. It places the church in the landscape within the background of the mountains; it guides one's gaze, upon entering, to the vastness of the sky.

The tall, closed facade toward the mountain

Access to the churchyard through the piazza
in Peccia marble

View of the western facade

The apse; on the facing page, the entire
internal space flooded with light

Facing page: the two flying buttresses
supporting the large glazed disk of the roof

Sketches by Mario Botta of the longitudinal
and cross sections

All formal gestures, as in the case of the house, have to do with the intensification of the reading of a
basic volume, but also with the articulation of an internal void—this place of gathering and collective
consciousness in which man comes in contact with the notion of the sacred. The solid presence of the
church raises its height to that of the mountains. Though firmly based on the ground, it aspires to the
sky. Spiritual values are spoken through form. There is no need for external references. The simple
expressive power of form transforms the building into a sign. The church is a symbol placed facing the
external world; gaze, movement, and worship are joined in a unified relation. The design plays with
contrasts. The massive stone wall is expressed through the succession of layers of stone slabs in
alternating strips of white Peccia marble and Riveo grey granite. Transparency and solidity, the material
and the spiritual, the sacred and the profane interweave in the composition of this perfectly designed
object, which uses subtle design gestures, geometrical order and the plasticity of mass to make this a
place for meditation and memory, remembrance and hope.

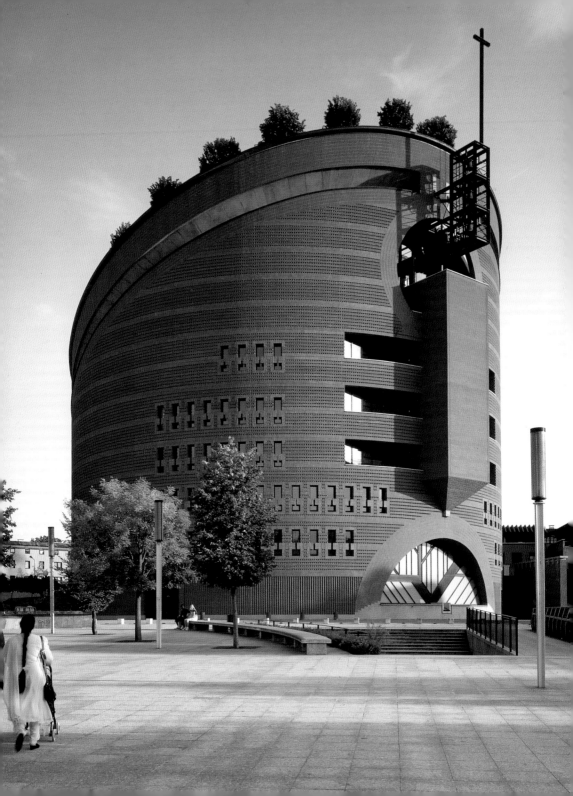

Cathedral of Evry

Evry, France, 1988-1995

This twentieth century Cathedral is situated in the Ville Nouvelle of Evry, a new suburb on the outskirts of Paris. "I have thought about the project for a house of God in the spirit of building the house of man," Mario Botta explains. A cathedral "…marks a pause, a moment of silence, an occasion for reflection and prayer for human beings faced with the rapid changes and contradictions of the modern-day city," he suggests.[4] Clad in brick, with its impressive cylindrical volume and skylight roof, the Cathedral marks the end of an apartment-block building on the main square of the suburb. The old idea of the cathedral not being an isolated element surrounded by open space, but rather a building placed side by side with houses, is thus brought back into play.

The basic volume is a truncated cylinder, circular in plan, with the same characteristic section as the Church in Mogno. The theme of the wall is celebrated once more. However, while in Mogno the interior was a void shaped by the emptying out of the mass of the volume, now the difference in scale is such that the wall cannot remain solid. It becomes empty, it defines void instead of mass. A double wall formed by the enclosure of two cylindrical volumes shapes the space this time. The external boundary contains the internal so that they become identical. This similarity seems to liberate the space in between, so that violations of the solid wall take place through extensions or subtractions. The wall becomes expressive. The Museum of Sacred Art placed at the side, with separate access from the outside, forces the wall to extrude. Surfaces become curved, the wall gains plasticity and stretches up to reach for the upper part of the truncated section.

Services, galleries and a circular ramp are located within the two boundaries. The ramp leads gradually from the entrance on the first floor down to the same point where the side-entrance is located. Space acquires theatrical qualities. The Cathedral becomes not only a place for individual worship and meditation; it is also a collective place. Movement takes part in

View from the southeast with the entrance; on the facing page, the taller part facing northwest

On the following pages: detail of the large openings in the northwestern facade, and the circular corridors inside the cathedral

the celebration of space; it creates spatial awareness as well as awareness of others. Movement laced with symbolic potential is uplifting—achieving contact with nature by reaching for the sky. The gallery space winds around the nave. Contained within the two boundaries, it opens up through the perforations in the internal wall to the grand void. The antithesis in scale, between the open and the secluded, is immense. Then, it extends outside along the walkway to the top and opens to the view. Trees placed at the perimeter form a crown at the top. The movement of leaves creates shadows. Their changing colors speak of the passing of time. A dialogue between the natural and the man-made is introduced.

Natural light from above floods the interior space. The section of the cylinder alternates between the solid and the transparent. Stained glass skylights at the sides of the triangular metal roof illuminate the interior. Light is a theme that talks about nature. Filtering through the trusses in the roof, light plays with shadow on the elaborate brick texture of the wall and warms the red color of the bricks to contrast with the black of the floor and the transparent wall behind the altar.

Composition becomes a play with antitheses: seclusion and openness, light and shadow, massive and transparent. Elements of intensity create a dynamic balance. Space and form become potent in their signification. The symbolic idea of nature intervenes. The sacred and the profane, the symbolic space of the church and the collective space of human gathering, unite. This is a place for the uplifting of the human spirit, for silence, and for reflection. The double wall resolves antitheses, making more prominent the reading of *oneness*.

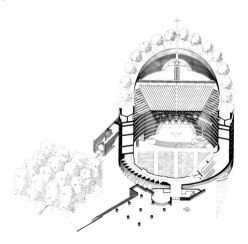

On the previous pages: the large interior space with view of the apse

The pattern and rhythm of the brick masonry

Open isometric

Facing page: the interior space with the openings for the galleries

San Francisco Museum of Modern Art

San Francisco, USA, 1989-1995

Set in the Yerba Buena area, at the foot of the Pacific Bell Building, the museum faces the Moscone Center park, while skyscrapers of downtown San Francisco form its backdrop. "I believe," Mario Botta says, "that today's museums are like yesterday's cathedrals: they are places of 'communication' where we can view works of art with the intention of assimilating and interpreting the messages they send us."[5] Three objectives set for the design of the museum also speak about what a museum is for the architect. The first stated that the museum should be an urban museum surrounded by natural light. A desire for the appreciation of art in a setting where light and shadow are allowed to take part in the ritual is a notion that addresses the ever-changing quality of time and the natural cycle of the seasons. The second aimed for an architecture that would permit visitors to understand simply and directly the spatial organization of the building. While orientation and points of reference speak about the interior, the third objective focuses on the museum with respect to the city. It sets as its goal the designing of a "styleless" building, a building with no ready-made identity. It aims, thus, for a permanent presence in a city continuously being transformed. It creates a symbolic form.

While the skyscrapers in the background reach for the sky, the museum rests its volume firmly on the ground. As if forming the base of a skyscraper, its orthogonal volumes expand horizontally and in recess. It is a steel structure while the walls are made from brick-clad prefabricated panels. Floors are staggered so that natural light illuminates all spaces, while the central light shaft becomes an enormous window that looks out over the city. Skylights aligned on the roof bring light into the galleries. Brick surfaces contrast with the powerful form of the skylight.

On the ground floor, which is more of a transitional area between the city and the museum, a large internal plaza contains a bookshop, cafeteria and auditorium. The first floor gallery houses the permanent collection, in a series of rather traditional gallery spaces inspired by Schinkel's nineteenth-century model of a sequence of rooms illuminated by natural light from above. Galleries on the second floor display photographs and works on paper. The top two floors, with their magnificent height, are for temporary exhibitions and exhibitions of large-scale contemporary art from the museum's permanent collection. Gallery space extends along the horizontal, bordered by solid walls, while the large void, the center of gravity, celebrates the vertical.

The museum stands out distinctively from its neighbors. Its mass is different. Whereas emphasis is usually placed on the vertical, the museum emphasizes the horizontal. Instead of the usual large glass surfaces and the repetitive rhythm of their openings, the building presents a silent face to the city. The brick cladding with its elegant detailing reveals little about the interior. It is a conscious choice. The museum chooses not to open up its interior to an outside view. The simplicity of its form, the clarity of its geometry, and the solidity of its mass indicate its difference and create a landmark.

The museum seen from the park

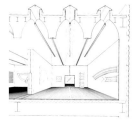

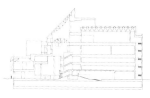

In ascending order: ground floor plan, second floor plan, longitudinal section, detail of the skylight for the exhibition rooms

Lateral view of the museum in the urban context of downtown San Francisco

What makes it such a powerful composition is not the innovation of new elements. The brick cladding, the long horizontal masses with their carefully designed openings, and the use of light from above are established elements in the formal vocabulary of Mario Botta. What surprises us most is the strength with which known elements are transformed in this context to gain new status. The truncated cylinder reappears. The powerful yet simple form of the San Giovanni Battista Church in Mogno is transformed here into total accentuation of the vertical axis. Emphasis on its grand opening, on this "Cyclop's eye," makes it a symbolic form. A point of reference for the interior becomes a symbol for the museum. The elegant brick cladding, on the other hand, is no longer just a cladding. It is a "mask" set in dialogue with urban complexity.

Skyline sketch

Landing of the main staircase

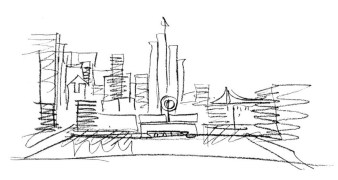

More than other buildings, a museum can be a container for human activity that needs the presence of spatial structure. Space, bounded by walls, needs to be read. The highly symmetrical plan of this museum requires no external references. Emphasis is on the central axis and the center of gravity of the composition. Continuities of boundaries and points of reference allow for this reading. The perception of space is immediate. A museum is a building about movement and pausing, about looking at art and being aware of the presence of others. The flow of movement from one gallery to the next culminates at the top. An ethereal bridge crosses over the great void, the transparent is in contradiction with the massive. Movement stands in suspension. The museum can now open up to the city. The silent face can become expressive once more.

Gallery

On the following pages: nocturnal view

Chapel of Santa Maria degli Angeli

Monte Tamaro, Ticino, Switzerland, 1990-1996

When Mario Botta was asked by a mountain ski-resort owner to build a chapel in memory of his deceased wife, he was left free to choose the exact place. This proved to be a difficult task. Restrictions on a given site present a well-known challenge for an architect, but complete freedom to locate a building anywhere in the vastness of the mountains presents a different problem altogether. It was finally the feeling of the particular site that made him decide that this was to be the location of the chapel. Like a line drawn from the peak of Monte Tamaro, leaving behind the ski facilities to its right and left, the building extends with the vastness of void created by the sharp mountain-face.

The building is a chapel, a place for meditation and thought, and at the same time a courtyard for open-air events. The volumetric composition is defined by one intensively linear element, a bridge, which dynamically materializes an axis passing over the top of the volume of the church. The chapel, made from porphyre stone, offers its cylindrical form as a base on which the bridge can rest. The linear bridge that is a stone-paved walkway leads the visitor to the edge of the cliff. Turning back and stepping down the staggered roof one can now enter the chapel. Walking through the covered walkway formed by the thick twin walls, by the repetitive rhythm of the circular windows and the partial views they offer heightened anticipation. If the first approach celebrates openness, the second, in contrast, prepares one for the secluded and the introspective. The process of approaching becomes a primary theme.

The darkness of the interior with the black cement-plastered walls is only interrupted by the rhythm of twenty-two windows placed at foot level, the white beams on the roof, and the light entering from above through the glazed steps of the promenade. The limits of interior space disappear; they are lost. Artist Enzo Cucchi's two cypresses interweave under the roof of the promenade, leading the visitor to the entrance; two blue hands stand in prayer at the sanctuary. Little poems mark each window; they offer consolation for the breathtaking view of the vastness of the void offered by the small windows.

The section of the cylinder is transformed to a staggered surface. Natural light penetrates the ordered perforations of the thick walls in such a way as to intensify their solidity. The antithesis between the interior

Facing page: the cylindrical volume of the church with the staircase leading to the intermediate level

Position of the chapel in the alpine context

and the exterior, evident in other churches by Mario Botta, ceases to exist. The internal and the external boundary become one. The intensity of the linear bridge is such that all other design gestures need to succumb. Axiality becomes the basic rule that organizes the whole. The building itself becomes a walkway, a promenade that almost leads one into the void.

Even though the chapel is small, its composition is dense in signification. The linearity of the bridge contrasts with the solid presence of the cylindrical base. Form becomes an expressive medium. Suspension and introversion, the vastness of the void as distinct from the solid presence of mountains, the earthly and the spiritual, the calling of the infinite, become transformed into space and form. The linear bridge extends both movement and gaze to the infinite, and the cylindrical enclosure of the chapel restricts movement and liberates feelings and thoughts.

The framing of the view offered by the covered walkway, the gradual disclosure of the magnificent view from the top of the promenade, or the partial view offered by the windows, underline the view's importance in the composition. These are not, however, pictorial aspects of a nice view. The building becomes a hymn to the mountains, a prayer for the eternal values of man. Contact with nature has become a symbol in itself. The symbolic upward movement, this characteristic element of Mario Botta's churches, is transformed in the chapel to man's movement towards the infinite. All other readings can now be condensed.

Facing page: the churchyard with the
convergence of the two accessways

Detail of the stepped roof and the access
to the belvedere; perspective sketch

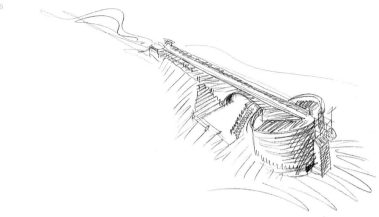

Chapel interior with frescoes by Enzo Cucchi   Detail of the stepped roofing with slender glass
                                                    inserts for diffused lighting inside the chapel

Jean Tinguely Museum

Basel, Switzerland 1993-1996

If Jean Tinguely's kinetic art structures use motion, sound, light, or water to expose the mechanisms and alienation of today's society, if they fear entropy and permanence, then Mario Botta's architecture, avoiding the ephemeral and the random, creates a strong contrast with them. This is a contrast that, instead of leading to tension, counterbalances art with architectural space and form. In the architect's words: "Works of art normally convey their message silently. Not Jean Tinguely's sculptures; they communicate through the sounds produced by their own movements. This slight difference may help us to understand the special conditions that works by this artist impose on a space."[6]

The museum is placed on a site where the river cuts an enormous swath through the city; a motorway bridge is located to the rear and a nineteenth-century park to the fore. Due to a decision to preserve the existing trees, the building is set on top of a big underground water tank. The static problem was significant. The underground tank had to be spanned by a roof structure supported by beams at either end, thereby creating exhibition spaces large enough to accommodate unusually big sculptures that need to be seen from all angles.

The design task is how to relate the museum to the various features of the context. Clad in pink Alsatian sandstone, each facade of the building answers the urban situation it confronts. A windowless facade faces the motorway-bridge. A wall separates the parking lot from the entrance. The visitor passes the portico, reminiscent of the characteristic form of the whole building, and enters the park. The facade on this side is completely open, characterized by a series of arches. The building faces the river with a strong formal element. A slightly curved glass bridge takes the visitor around the magnificent river view, before he enters the galleries. "Thus, the museum's first exhibit becomes the river," explains Mario Botta, demonstrating "how a commission to design a museum for a city can result in a part of the city becoming an exhibit in its own right. Functional features interact with other more symbolic components of the design so that visitors are able in turn to interact with the context."[7]

On the ground floor, the museum consists of one large space, which can be divided by sliding partitions, hidden in the depth of the beams, into five different compartments. To enter the galleries, the visitor has to first pass over the bridge that leads to the upper floor. Thus, the exhibition spaces are actually first entered on the mezzanine floor from which the spacious ground floor galleries can be viewed from above. One can now descend to the ground floor. A kind of "promenade architecturale" takes visitors around the building and allows them to appreciate not only the exhibits, but also the building and the view in a sequence. If orientation and the ability to easily grasp the whole spatial structure were important in the design of the San Francisco Museum, movement becomes primary in this museum, it becomes part of the museum experience.

The formal composition marks a departure in Mario Botta's poetics. His architecture, in its maturity, can accept significant transformations. This is not a composition of primary volumes, gradually hollowed out,

Southern facade of the museum overlooking
the Rhine

nor a composition of an autonomous object. Reminiscent of Louis Kahn's Kimbell Art Museum, the museum's form is not conceived all at once, but is characterized by the repetition of a structural system. Context intervenes. It upsets geometrical order, transforms each particular facade, and introduces one of the main design features: the ramp. Form does not hesitate to borrow from the real world, to be referential. The metaphor of a boat shapes the bridge. Yet, this is unmistakably a Mario Botta building: in the grandness of the rhythm of the apses, in the elegance and power of the formal gestures, in the play between closed and open, between solid and transparent, in its intense dialogue with the context, and in the surprise of the formal elaboration of the ramp. It constitutes a generous, well-balanced and ordered form that allows its content to be exhibited and expressed in contrast.

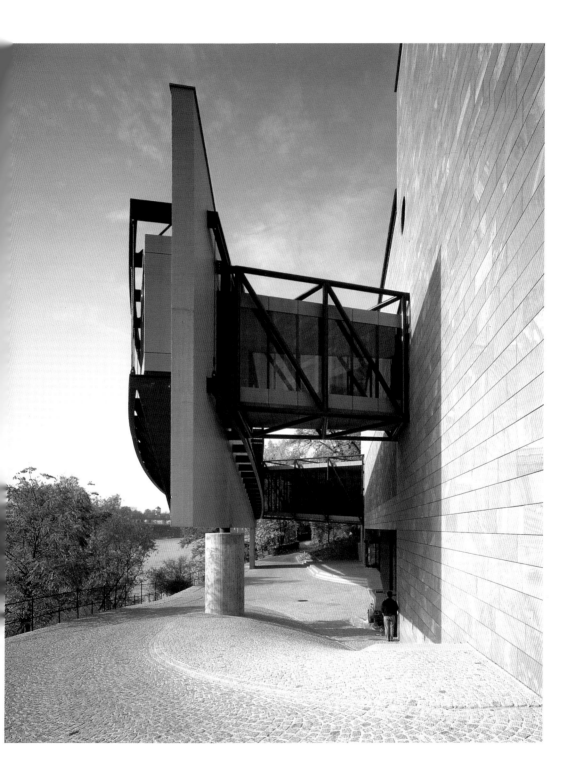

On the previous pages: the two connection points of the building and detail of the metal support structure of the walkway

The glazed corridor overlooking the Rhine

Plan and sections

View of the western facade from the park, with the portico and the large recessed windows

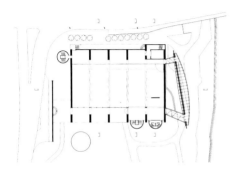

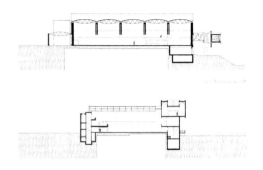

Ground floor interior, with views toward the
first floor gallery and the park; perspective
sketches

Municipal Library

Dortmund, Germany, 1995-1999

The first prizewinner in an international competition, the building stands on a 7,000 square meter plot and has a gross area of 14,130 square meters. It consists of two volumes. One, an upside down truncated half-cone, all in glass that houses the reception area, the library catalogues, and the reading rooms. The other, a long orthogonal building treated as a closed linear mass, stepped like a ziggurat at the back, for offices and storage, that sets a boundary and marks a limit for the plot, while the cone opens up to the public square and faces the railway station.

The geometry introduces an antithesis taken up also by the structure: the linear block, with red Swedish quartzite cladding, is in reinforced concrete, while in the cone floors are supported by reinforced concrete and the glass surface by a boldly dimensioned steel structure. The cone is a high-tech building all in steel and double glass walls with an electronically moved system of *brise-soleil* for protection from the sun. It is the first time Mario Botta uses glass to completely envelope a building. However, contrary to what is expected, glass is not a mere cladding, an outer epidermis for the building. The glass facade reveals its structure. The glass and steel interweave, becoming a face for the building.

The two volumes stand in contradiction—an antithesis in shape and volume, in material as well as in use. The composition is characterized by tension: the public areas of the building contrast with the private ones, the cone with the linear volume, the transparency of the glass with the solidity of the stone cladding, and the serenity of the rhythmical repetition of the thin windows in the linear building with the tension of the glass structure in the cone. It is a contrast chosen deliberately in order to emphasize difference between the compact limits of the historic town and the empty space just outside of it. In Mario Botta's words: "The design aims to consolidate the urban front of the city at the exit to the railway station. That is why the new building is divided into two distinct parts: a massive austere red stone linear volume re-establishing the walled front and a truncated glass cone, protruding from the alignment, to be used as the reading room and leisure facility."[8]

This is not a composition based on the primacy of one notion. It is, instead, based on a distinction between pairs of notions. It thus marks a departure. Unlike Mario Botta's other buildings, where one or more volumes are treated in a similar way, the glass cone at the Dortmund Library dictates a different treatment of space. Floor surfaces are kept at a distance; they let the glass structure evolve without interfering. While in the half cylinder of the Mediatheque at Villeurbanne, the interior void created a centripetal *point of reference*, the transparent glass in the Dortmund Library becomes a centrifugal surface, a continuous *surface of reference* in the view of the city. The Library becomes extroverted. The transparent surface wraps up part of the roof in a sharp corner. But, instead of having a glass roof as in other cases where the cylindrical volume is sectioned, the roof is now opaque. The cone celebrates the surface that bounds the volume.

Overall view

However, by departing from the rule, the building exhibits all the qualities of the canon. If we take, for example, the treatment of the glass facade, instead of the glass being a skin, it acquires texture, structure, and even a kind of transparent massiveness. It is not a cladding of the vertical, a dressing of surfaces. It expands on three dimensions; it acquires volumetric qualities. What we have is a glass volume, not glass surfaces. Even when worked in glass, the architecture of Mario Botta is architecture of the mass.

Eastern facade

Nocturnal view of the transparent conical
volume of the library

On the previous pages: nocturnal view
showing the transparency of the building and
the geometry of the structure

Axonometric

Detail views of the metal structure of the public
space with the anchoring and the glazing

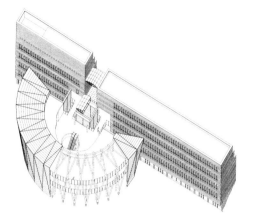

Cumbre de las Americas Monument

Santa Cruz de la Sierra, Bolivia, 1996

A monument is a building for memory and remembrance, a structure with potential for signification. Its form is there to express content, to speak about something else. Form and space become the medium. However, they do not have to speak the language of symbolism in order to be meaningful. Their formal means, in their abstraction, has the power to express without being literal. A monument is erected in order to remind. Form and the shaping of space can play this role.

This monument was erected to commemorate the summit on sustainable growth that took place in Santa Cruz, the second city of Bolivia, on December 6, 1996. The idea was to create a gate for a huge park close to the center of the city. It consists of two corner towers, standing 22 meters high, that bring to mind images of Mayan guardian figures. The structure is in concrete, clad in red brick. Each tower forms a corner with two double walls that contain staircases at their ends. On the second floor and on the roof, viewing terraces have been created. The corner is emphasized. It is transformed into a kind of a "head" on the top, adding to the anthropomorphic image of the building. Part of the walls on the ground level is removed, revealing two grand round columns also clad in brick.

The large urban park with the two corner towers

The formal gesture departs from the simple treatment of the corner. It creates allusions. What is emptied on the ground level is put back on top to make a kind of turret. Each facade seen in isolation creates tension in the way it stands slightly off-balance. Tension is deliberate. Stability is recovered only when the two walls are seen together and the corner is read. The treatment of the corner offers only a base for formal elaboration. Composition plays with the double image, evident not only in the double walls. The two towers, standing at each corner on opposite sides, are set in a dialogue. Each facade, slightly incomplete, each one in need of its twin at the other end in order to be read in full. What appears as a formal play is, in reality, strongly enriched with signification, for the image created by the facade speaks a symbolic language.

The two towers stand as the realized parts of a virtual wall that protects the park from the noise of the city. They mark the ends of a wall that does not exist in reality, but is only implied. Their distance is compensated for and their *oneness* restored not only through their apparent similarity. A walkway connects the two towers marked by twenty-three little fountains on the ground. On the top, a laser

beam comes out from the porthole 'eyes' on the turrets, and connects them once more, in a virtual way this time.

The color of the brick contrasts nicely with the trees. Staircases take the visitor gradually to the top. Views are revealed through the many little holes punctuating the texture of the wall. Movement, space, and form come together in a powerful composition. This is not an abstract form to be deciphered and read. It is a building that needs to be explored, to be experienced—a building that brings together feelings and thoughts. It transforms the experience of walking in the park, of entering the world of nature, of leaving behind the sounds of the city, into a built form. It is a gate between the natural and the artificial, between the world of the park and that of the city. It is also a building to evoke memories, a monument to remind us of the need to gradually transform nature, of the importance of recovering space for survival.

A narrow canal with a series of fountains
connects the two towers

Facing page: the perforated facade of one of
the towers

The open accessway with the stairs at its end

Exterior perimeter view

Landing on the first floor terrace

Light and shadow effects created by the irregular pattern of the brick; insertion of the terraces between the two walls

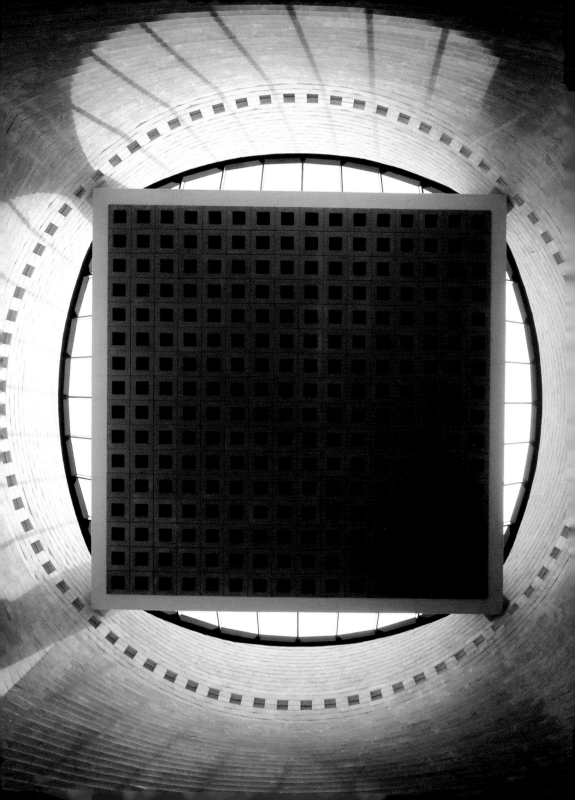

Cymbalista Synagogue and Jewish Heritage Center

Tel Aviv, Israel, 1996-1998

Two impressive, truncated cones standing on a low linear base take the visitor by surprise. This unusual twin form houses a synagogue and a cultural center for Tel Aviv University. The two halls are identical. Neither of them dominates the other. They constitute two squares separated by the spacious entrance area, overlooking each other through big openings. Gradually, moving to the roof, the square form becomes cylindrical by careful extrusion from its sides. The roof is another square inscribed in the circle, while the four remaining parts become skylights that open to the sky.

The synagogue hall, the religious space, is no different from the public hall. Emphasis on the twin nature of the building is deliberate. Solitude and gathering, religious worship and cultural exchange can take place side by side, can be expressed by the same form. The enigma of the twin form can now be deciphered.

Spatial clarity, stone, memories of the vernacular buildings of the architect's home area, create a space for emotions to evolve. This is a building for meditation, a place where one can rest from the hustle and bustle of daily life. The geometric clarity of the spatial structure, the openness to the sky, the grand scale and, at the same time, the intimacy and the serenity of the detailing, give this building its place among the other religious buildings by Mario Botta.

Pietra di prun from the region of Verona, a calcite and sedimentary stone, 15 cm thick, is used for the external surfaces, while the interior is clad in *pietra dorata*, a sandstone that gives the interior a more finished appearance. Concrete structure and stone are built in combination to give shape to this interesting form. While brick or stone cladding with its elegant detailing was used in previous buildings by Mario Botta in order to emphasize the materiality of the surface, or to distinguish the front, now the material gains a volumetric quality. It is not just a cladding; it has mass. The solidity of the wall in contrast with the lightness of the roof becomes the main feature. Thick stone slabs are used to shape the volume. The gradual extrusion of each series of slabs transforms the square shape into a circle, a gesture that brings to mind the powerful transformation of an ellipsis in the plan to a perfect circle on the truncated rooftop of the Church in Mogno. Yet, while in Mogno the theme was the mass of the wall, now the wall is again, although thick, a surface.

The building has a base, a rectangle that delineates and defines. The base relates to the ground; it is a border and a limit. It also creates a front. Two cylindrical columns emphasize the axis of symmetry between the twin forms. Symmetrical glass edges imply double axes of symmetry of the protruding volumes. As soon as the base stops, the previously contained square volumes explode. Their walls become transformed. Edges gradually lose their sharpness. Layer by layer, the new form is revealed.

A square within a circle gives form to the roof and the skylights that illuminate the synagogue interior

On the following pages: the main entrance facade of the synagogue and cultural center

The wall distances itself from the ceiling. The square reappears, contained now by the circle.

The vertical is accentuated and at the same time retained. The uplift of the wall is strongly controlled by the horizontal roof. The upward movement of the truncated section of other churches by Mario Botta, has given place to the serenity of the horizontal line. The verticality of space is only internalized. The twin form is even more emphasized in its duality by the horizontality of the exterior. Space opens up to the sky by its inverted conical form, and still remains firmly based on the ground. If the search for the divine is symbolized by the vertical axis, the strong base and the horizontal skyline of the synagogue turn its referentiality back to the human condition.

Facing page: the geometry of a tower, ascending from the square to the circle

Detail of the stepped stone masonry layers of the two towers

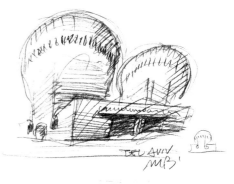

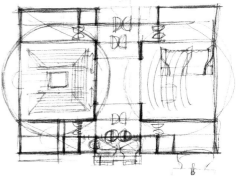

The entrance hall and foyer; working sketch
of the plan and the perspective

Facing page: interior of the synagogue with
view of the auditorium

Wooden Model of the Borromini Church San Carlo alle Quattro Fontane

Lugano, Switzerland, 1999

A life-size model of the cross-section of the San Carlo alle Quattro Fontane Church in Rome was created on the occasion of the 400th anniversary of Francesco Borromini's birth in Bissone, in the region of Ticino. The model, 35 meters high, was made of 35,000 wooden planks, each 4.5 cm thick, mounted modularly with a separation of 1 cm, and held together with steel cables fixed to a steel frame weighing 90 tons. Even though the initial idea was to have it floating in the lake, the model was finally placed on a square platform anchored a few meters from the shore, at the end of the promenade on the lake in Lugano.

The real church, a small but very distinctive building placed between houses, almost lacks an exterior. With only a corner of it visible and detailed, the church cannot be defined from the outside. The interior of the church is, on the other hand, worked-out in full detail. Its section, characteristic of Baroque architecture, is elegant and refined, with protrusions, recesses, and decorations. Its elaboration with beautifully worked-out proportions, an exemplar of the notion of proportion in architecture, is the most distinguished feature of the building.

The model celebrates this section. The scale is one to one, the material is wood. Little oblong wooden strips recreate the form, always reminding the spectator through their separation and discontinuity, that this is indeed a representation. The outside surface is presented as a blank box. It is a box painted black that emphasizes the antithesis between the elaborate interior and the bland exterior—a black box that envelopes the magnificent section and contrasts with the horizon seen from afar.

The model is a translation of reality into discourse about the real. A new boundary delineates space. Shape and detailing remain the same. The reproduction is exact. However, the material is different, ephemeral. Space is recreated by mass translated into another medium. The wooden structure becomes only the means. The slight distancing between the wooden strips allows light to violate the solidity of the mass. The solid is transformed into the transparent. The real and its representation stand in suspension. Thought and creative inspiration, rigorous measurement and artisanship, mind, soul and hand all combine, keeping only to the essentials.

The model is not only a representation. It is also a statement about the very essence of architecture, space, and form. It is a statement about the creation of form by the shaping of the wall, about the unique quality of the wall, and the formation of space by the elaboration of mass. It is a

Internal section view and cupola detail

statement about the notion of negative space, about absence (of the exterior) and powerful presence (of the interior), a translation of reality into a different language, a language perhaps more abstract, but equally strong and meaningful.

The model is also an act of remembrance. Its presence is symbolic. Instead of being an abstract sign, the model celebrates the birth of a great architect through direct reference to his work. Meaning is condensed. While the real is whole, the representation is sectioned. While the real is contained within, surrounded by urban fabric, the representation floats on the water. The mountains in the background take part in the play of signification. Their presence stands for the topography of the area itself, alludes to the native land of the celebrated architect. The geographical reference remains implied. The whole is spoken by the part. Lit in the darkness of the night with its warm light, contained as it is by its black box, the model gains an almost mystical status. It becomes a statement about the power of architectural form, the power of architecture itself.

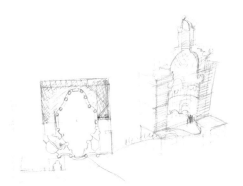

View of the platform with the wooden structure on the Lugano lakefront

Facing page: view of the cutaway facade

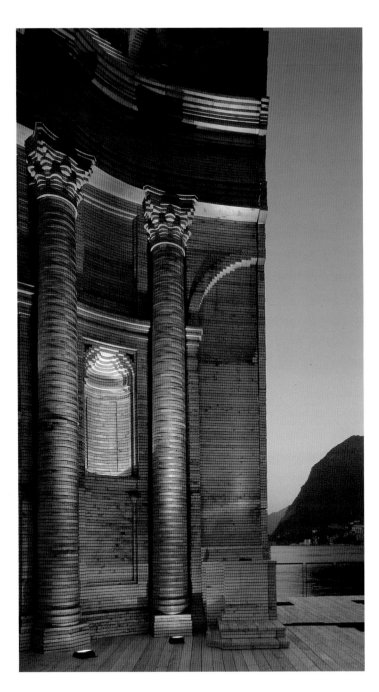

Close-ups of the space and the architectural
details reproduced with pine planks

Church at Malpensa Airport 2000

Milan, Italy, 1998-

More so than in any other place, space in airports is transient. We are used to airports being, in architectural terms, open, transparent, huge, impersonal. In antithesis to this, the hypothesis for this new church in Malpensa Airport, Milan, was to offer the traveler an alternative space, a space that would be introverted instead of open, secluded instead of unlimited, with clear borders defined by stone walls instead of the usual transparency offered by airport lounges. Connected to the International Departures Building by a walkway 14 meters off the ground, the new church appears like a flower in stone, a clover-leaf. It is an autonomous object, a place that opens only to the sky, a place for meditation and comfort for all religions, a place for the international traveler to calm down and reflect.

A triangle with cut-off corners, surrounded by three semi-cylinders all inscribed in a circle, form the overall shape. The elongated cylinders, cut by a 45-degree plane, like huge organ-pipes, reach up to a height of 31 meters off the ground. Their sections are transparent all-glass roofs that let the light accentuate the texture of the walls and the contrast in height between the central core and the cylinders. Entry is from above. On the four levels below the entrance, the building houses the chapel on the first floor and then offices, a multi-use room and technical spaces are located on three more floors. The triangular shape forming the base at the center rises to a height of 14.5 meters. Vertical circulation takes place through one of the cylinders, while the other two are dedicated to the pulpit and the altar. The structure is in reinforced concrete, and the exterior walls and part of the interior walls are clad in red Verona stone.

The wall, the handling light, the entrance procedure, and the emphasis on the vertical element are the characteristics of any church by Mario Botta, and the new church of Malpensa Airport is indeed a celebration of all these themes. However, as if form does not hesitate this time to look to nature for inspiration, it also marks a departure from the formal composition of his other churches.

The circular shape of the wall multiplied by three exaggerates the strength of the geometry. The primary solid of other buildings has been transformed into a complex volume. Yet this is again one object, not a composition of many. Similarity and repetition of the cylinders is not only formal. It carries within it references to the external world. If contact with nature in an idealistic form is a theme to be found in all of Mario Botta's churches, expressed by the play with natural light or the openness to the sky, this time idealized nature gives form its shape and meaning. As if imitating a petrified flower, form duplicates the morphological essence of the organic, its structure, and the logic of form generation.

The verticality of the three truncated cylinders, the massiveness of the stone-clad wall, the openness of the cylinders to the sky, the gradual procedure of descending from the bustle of the outside world to a world of calm and serenity, create a place with symbolic power. The formal qualities of this new church move discreetly beyond significance towards the realms of signification. This man-made stone flower made for prayer becomes meaningful to the traveler, without having to sacrifice the power of the abstraction of its form.

Cutaway model and working sketch

Chapter Four

A Matter of Scale

Mario Botta is an architect that moves across scale easily. He does not hesitate to handle both the minute and the large. Size is not a problem as long as the building can answer the questions set by the site and program. Indeed, the potential for signification might be greater for a building of small stature, since its form can be read immediately. On the other hand, Mario Botta succeeds in giving his large-scale buildings a strong identity, so that they are unmistakably his. Yet, a large-scale building presents a departure from the rule. It cannot be so easily defined as an object. Form cannot be as autonomous as it is on a small scale. The large-scale building already has a presence by virtue of its size. However, form-giving is more demanding than this. Gestures need to be redefined.

In urban conditions, the large-scale building needs to be dealt with on an urban scale. Design has to provide an answer to the urban situation. The urban fabric, the castle, the river, the new and the old parts of the city, limits and borders, street lines and elevations, and the scale of neighboring buildings, are the existing problems that the large-scale building has to face. The city both shapes and is shaped by the building. A courtyard becomes the point where the public and the private meet—where they come together. The city becomes

Swisscom building, Bellinzona

enclosed by the Caimato Office Building in Lugano-Cassarate (1986-1993). A huge courtyard facing the castle makes the Swisscom Building in Bellinzona (1988-1999) an urban reference.

Then, there is the matter of giving scale, rhythm. Sometimes the breaking of scale is necessary in order to bring the building closer to its neighbors, as is the case with the Banca del Gottardo in Lugano. Or, it is sometimes necessary to scale the building down so that its presence does not upset existing urban relations. This is what the Museum for Modern and Contemporary Art and Cultural Center in Rovereto (1988-93/2001) does. Sometimes the opposite gesture is needed; the composition has to create a presence, to give form to the site, as is the case of the Offices and Housing at Maastricht (1990-2000), or the Scientific College in Città della Pieve (1993-2000). In the Residence Settlement at Novazzano (1988-1992) and in the Row Houses and Redaeli Villa at Bernareggio (1991-1997/99), the problem is how to bring together a series of identical units and combine them into a complex composition of a higher order. In an elegant way, each unit remains defined and yet incomplete; it needs its neighbor in order to be read as a whole. Scale is, indeed, a matter of architecture.

Caimato Office Building

Lugano-Cassarate, Switzerland, 1986-1993

A large-scale building is a building that first of all has to respond to the urban situation. Its mass creates urban fronts; its horizontal expansion delineates urban blocks. A building of this size sets an intriguing problem for the architect, for it cannot easily be defined as a simple gesture. Size justifies presence but does not detract from the need for image.

This large office building is situated along the tree-lined bank of the River Cassarate in Lugano. The complex takes the form of a U-shaped block with an inner courtyard. The two parts on the long sides house offices, while the central, connecting block is assigned mainly to circulation. The triangular ending of the two corners on the side blocks opens up the courtyard to the city. A delicate treatment of triangular geometry with right angle corners through distancing and little cuts, signifies the solidity of the end points of the blocks. Having established that the building is firmly standing on the ground, the long sides can now be emptied. A series of round columns reveals a glass surface that gradually steps forward in the first two floors, creating a covered space for the colonnade. The connecting block opens up through a grand void placed on the axis of symmetry of the whole complex: ample emptying out of the volume reveals a view towards the mountains. A small cylinder with emphasis on the vertical dimension is also placed off the axis at one side.

The building, which is clad in brick, with alternating horizontal zoning, is straightforward and serene in composition. Circulation is placed at the corners, leaving large open surfaces for office expansion. The scale is such that it calls for an urban approach. The long sides, which follow the existing street lines, create strong elevations. The theme of opening the building to the city by creating a large empty space within its volume—the theme, that is, of designing a void—reappears. However, the body of the building

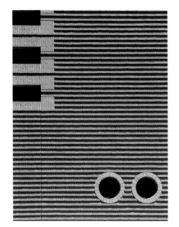

can no longer be a primary solid as in the case of the Centro Cinque Continenti in Lugano-Paradiso. The difference in scale is immense. The linear blocks delineate the internal void. There is no difference in the treatment of the internal and external elevations. What is contained by the brick surfaces is urban space, which also belongs to the city. The initial idea of placing some kind of pergola over the courtyard and letting the plants grow was dropped. Had this idea been realized, it would have brought the project much closer to the ideas Mario Botta had already experimented with in the past. On this occasion, what is today an urban block, would have come closer to an object volumetrically defined in such a way as to intensify the reading of the built and the empty space as a whole. The pergola would have contributed not only to spatial quality, but would have added to the underlying signification.

Detail of the brick masonry   View of the courtyard

The alternating rhythm of the vertical and circular openings and of horizontal slits and the variations in the delicate horizontal zoning of the bricks, which constitute elements of the personal and yet universal vocabulary of the compositional style of Mario Botta, are present here. The volumetric definition departs from the rule of a primary object that is emptied out. The size of the building cannot allow for a gesture of this kind. At the same time, however, the architect succeeds in handling a complex of large scale in such a way that it becomes an urban project. This is a project that gives shape to this part of the city in the way it follows lines, defines edges, creates openings to the view and introduces rhythm with its facades; it is a project that creates urbanity.

The open front with the two slanting wings

Facing page: detail of the portico facing the
Cassarate River

Residence Settlement

Novazzano, Ticino, Switzerland, 1988-1992

The complex is a small estate developed to provide subsidized housing, a proper *siedlung* of one hundred dwellings, situated not far from the village of Novazzano, in the lower part of Ticino. These low-cost, four-story apartment blocks are organized in a U-shaped block on the upper part of the site. The block surrounds a paved yard which lies on top of an underground parking-area, while the two wings form the opposite sides of a second open courtyard. This yard, on ground level, larger and grassed over, is the children's main play area. A bridge connects the lower courtyard to a small shopping center. The estate is entered on the ground-floor from the back. It opens up to reveal a covered portico created through a succession of round openings on vertical planes giving a surprising visual effect. The block with the portico forms the third closed side of the courtyard, while the fourth side remains open to view.

Mario Botta translates his experience of detached housing into a collective housing scheme. Features such as top-floor loggias, covered porticos, and terraces set back in the facades are also employed in this scheme. Since the size and construction standards of the apartments were already prescribed, the architect focuses, instead, on the transitional spaces between interior and exterior, on the positioning of porticos and loggias.

The typology of the apartments varies on each floor, while the block set farthest to the south houses a series of duplexes. The linear blocks are formally divided into smaller units with gardens at the back: a rhythm of vertical and horizontal elements, of buttresses and recesses, of protected terraces appearing as subtractions in the volume, of intermediate spaces opening up through cylindrical skylights to the sky, and of symmetrically delineated openings forming the facades. The initial idea of cladding the volumes in brick was dropped for reasons of cost. Instead, for the first time, the architect uses color to render the facades. The strong color scheme in reds and blues, reminiscent of Bruno Taut, adds to the character of the place, emphasizing the composition of the volumes. Salmon pink is used for the outer facades, ochre for the recessed volumes, and blue for the intermediate service areas, in an attempt, in the architect's words, "to give" to a popular housing project "a dignified status."[1]

The problem of designing a *siedlung* is not only one of typology or of distinctions between public and private realms; the problem of endless repetition of identical units also needs to be addressed in terms of design. The design of this complex in Novazzano succeeds in both aims. Units are ordered into linear blocks that bound the open space. Facades gain volumetricity; shadows and color underline the contours of extruding volumes. Formal elements are combined in twin form to create the impression of a gradual ordering of units into larger clusters. Repetition becomes a formal play with order; each unit taking part in a larger class of elements, which, in turn, are also ordered to a higher degree. Vertical elements on the facades support the long horizontal extrusion from the upper floor. A recessed linear backbone penetrates the whole series. The scheme chooses to be slightly ambiguous, making it difficult

to distinguish if this is a series of detached houses or if it is a linear block volumetrically broken into smaller units. In ordered variety, the facades can, at the same time, border the ample public spaces as well as open up to the view. The problem of repetition has been resolved in formal terms.

The volumetric pattern of the facade overlooking the plaza

Plan and section of the housing estate.

View of the settlement and the bridge leading
to the shopping center across the road

On the following pages: view from the large
plaza positioned amidst the housing units,
open toward the plains of "Mendrisiotto"

Swisscom Building

Bellinzona, Switzerland, 1988-1999

Located in Bellinzona, on the outskirts of the city, this large building, clad in brick, houses the head offices of the state telecommunications company. Grand in scale, it becomes the focal point in the area. It defines a limit, an actual border for the city as it stands facing the Bellinzona Castle and opens its inner courtyard in this direction. It is a square building, approximately 100 meters long on each side, while part of its fourth side is missing. A circular inner courtyard is inscribed in the square. Where the opening in the big inner court is located, special treatment of the corner occurs. The corner becomes an independent building, an orthogonal volume inscribed in a semi-cylinder which houses a variety of public services and leisure facilities, as well as a large hall and a cafeteria open to the general public. The building marks the entrance to the courtyard, a huge inner piazza used for recreation, where a pool was originally planned instead of grass. The main entrance to the complex, placed on the corner further up, becomes accentuated by a dramatic vertical cut and a long bridge that crosses the courtyard on the diagonal, pointing also in the direction of the Castle.

Like most of the public buildings by Mario Botta built on this scale, this is an urban project. It creates a microcosm, while, at the same time, it responds to the city. This is a building that is an autonomous entity as well as a project for the city. It is not only its opening toward the Bellinzona Castle, or the public use of its large inner court that gives it urbanity. It is the way it defines the edge of the city, the way it responds to the immediate surroundings and those beyond that integrate this large complex. It maintains its own strong identity but at the same time initiates a dialogue with the urban fabric.

The interior is organized in a classical plan. The corners, as always, are geometrically defined. They are occupied by vertical circulation, while horizontal circulation, running along the sides of the square, gives access to offices on both sides, facing either toward the outside or toward the inner courtyard. A void that continues through all floors, with a skylight at the top, penetrates each corner. The upper floor is recessed, thus defining the perimeter of the square, which gives way to a kind of top-floor promenade for an appreciation of the view. Like most of Mario Botta's large public buildings, the building is clad in brick, with horizontal zoning, while the rhythm of the vertical windows is emphasized by the whiteness of their protruding window sills.

This project is, however, different from the Caimato Office Building. This is an object that is conceived all at once; a huge square that is emptied out. The void is clearly defined in its geometry: it is a large circle in the plan—a large, void cylinder with negative volume. As in the case of Centro Cinque Continenti, Mario Botta brings the city into the building. The primary distinction between closed private spaces and open public ones, which characterizes all of his public buildings, is also evident here. In addition, the distinction between the solid and the void, between what is built and what is left as a purposely-designed void, is always present. The scale of the building interferes, but not to such a degree as to upset the logic of composition. Scale will be resolved in urban terms. The building is to mark the

Partial view of the curved facade and the portico

Perspective sketch and view of the circular
internal courtyard; the bridge aligned with the
diagonal axis of the edifice leads to the main
entrance

end of the city, to delineate the border, to create a focal point in dialogue with the Castle. The problem of a large-scale building is that it will not let composition deviate from the primary rule. The rule will again be present in order to define the volume, to handle variations in the facade, to accentuate the corner, or to materialize the main axis.

The courtyard with a view of the cylindrical volume that contains the multipurpose hall, positioned as the conclusion of the office block

Interior (with reception area) at the corner of the building, with the large four-story void

Facing page: the external emergency stairwell is the conclusion of the other extremity of the building; in the foreground, the platform roofing defines the entrance zone for the courtyard

Row Houses and Villa

Bernareggio, Italy, 1991-1997/99

In the residential area of the Brianza countryside, in Lombardy, north of Milan, ten houses are placed one next to the other in perfect order. In their exact alignment, they form an axis that runs from the town toward the north. The sequence of houses concludes with a single house, the Villa, a building with a curved facade at the rear.

The ten houses create a linear block constituted by the repetition of the same orthogonal volume, the same primary solid. Parts are subtracted from each solid, and symmetry does not dominate any longer. Cuts on the surface are well-ordered by an intervening element. However, this element is not emphasized, but only vaguely implied in the composition. Each cut organizes an intermediate space, a space connecting the inside to the outside. There are no windows, only large glass surfaces where the volume has been hollowed out. As if ordered by double articulation, what is seen as a serene, well-ordered facade from some distance, reveals at closer inspection a kind of tension created by the placement of the cuts. This tension on each particular facade, on each one of the houses, results in an interesting rhythm through the repetition of one element that only becomes complete with the addition of the adjoining ones.

The composition terminates with the volume of the Villa. Its size is significant, its height slightly greater than that of the houses. While the houses face the road, the villa faces in the opposite direction and thus opens up to the landscape on the other side. Clad also in brick, it looks like another linear block in close proximity to the houses. And yet, one has only to look at the rear to realize that what appears to be a linear element is in reality a dissected cylinder which has been cut in half once and then cut in half again. What remains maintains a reference to the cylinder, for the cylindrical surface of the original volume is still evident. Two strong pillars carry the weight of the roof, while a large

View of the residential complex   Detail view of the openings in the villa facade

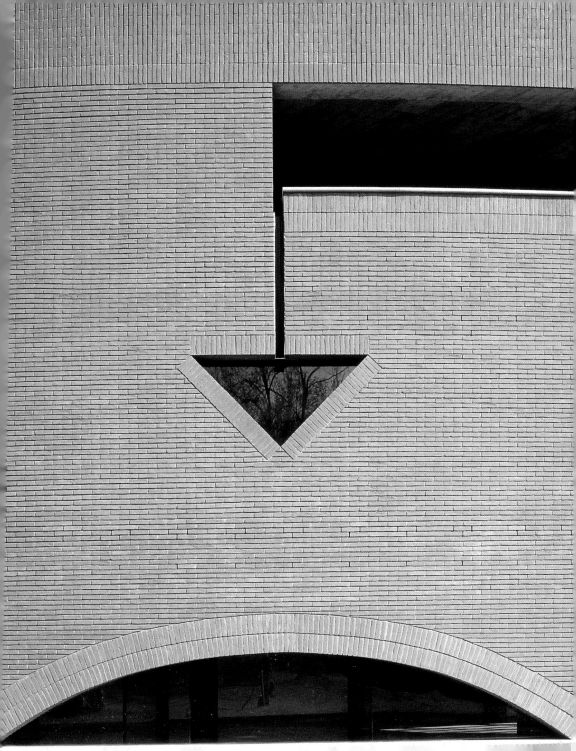

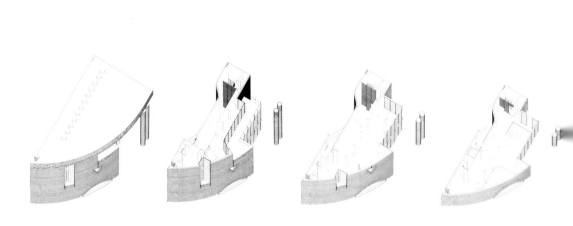

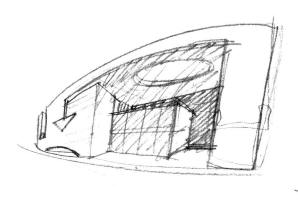

Facing page: axonometric drawings of different
levels; nocturnal view

Working sketch of the main facade of the villa,
characterized by geometric openings

hollowing out of the volume exposes large glass surfaces to the landscape. An open staircase on the linear facade gives direct access to the second floor. The triangular shape of its recess terminates the volumetric subtractions that define the series of houses.

Since the external surface is so strong in its geometry, the interior can be made freer. The ground floor of the Villa is devoted to recreation and houses the indoor swimming pool. Daytime activities are allocated to the first floor, while the second floor houses private space. Cuts create covered transitional spaces on the exterior. Voids connect all floors visually. The geometry of the interior is fluid and has broken free from the ordered discipline of the symmetrical axis. In contrast, the reading of the external surface compensates for the restless interior. And yet, this is a surface that is never complete. Symmetry has been violated, negated. A triangular cut on the curved surface hints at what could be implied as an axis of symmetry. The gesture is only a partial one, a limited one, for it cannot refute the absence of an axis of symmetry in the volume. What constitutes the complex volume, its surfaces, and their geometry is there to relate to the landscape; the linear presents a limit and creates a sharp edge on one side, while the curved one opens up on the other side. The difference between the two is there to relate the Villa to the houses and the complex as a whole to the landscape. The matter of scale can once more accept subtle interpretations, can interweave with the landscape and the site, can be an issue treated with careful variations in space and form.

The large covered terrace on the second floor and, below, the swimming pool area on the ground floor

Facing page: the internal void adjacent to the living area permeates two levels, and is accentuated by a series of skylights

Gerbio Residences

Monte Carasso, Bellinzona, Switzerland, 1992-1996

In a small town near Bellinzona, characterized by Luigi Snozzi's town-planning work for the rejuvenation of the area, Mario Botta was invited to design low-cost housing on a site close to the old restored convent. Clad in light gray concrete blocks, the complex houses thirty apartments and consists of two blocks: an orthogonal one with small cylindrical extrusions and another with a curved side that points to a sharp edge, connected by an open-air corridor. The two volumes are brought together by the use of a large canopy. The canopy, a painted white metal grid structure covered by transparent polycarbonate, is the main feature of the building, while a cylindrical volume for vertical circulation marks the end of the open space.

The theme of the courtyard, of an enclosed public space that opens up to the city, previously explored by the architect, appears once more. However, a different element is now introduced. The transparent covering brings to mind the Centro Cinque Continenti, and its character as the courtyard in a composition of distinct volumes might bring to mind, though on a different scale, the Caimato Office Building. This time, though, the canopy offers an independent identity to the courtyard and, at the same time, declares its role as the go-between.

This is not a unitary composition, as in the case of the Home for the Elderly in Novazzano. It is, instead, a composition of two equal, yet distinct volumes. The volumetric definition does not start from one primary solid gradually hollowed out in order to create intermediate spaces and to reveal the interior to the outside. The two volumes play an equal role in the synthesis, brought together by the use of a third element. The intermediate space is not a space created by the subtraction of a larger volume any longer. It is not an element in itself and it is still part of the overall articulation of the mass. Even though its proportions and materials are carefully treated, it remains an outside space, a space that belongs equally to the complex and to the external world.

The two housing blocks are positioned around a covered plaza

The rectilinear western streetfront of the edifice

The orthogonal volume follows the street line, while the curved one opens up to the free surroundings. Subtle formal manipulations of the endings of the two volumes add to the richness of the space. The courtyard opens to the view at one side as the curved building stands more to the back, while the elongated side of the orthogonal volume protects the open space from the street. Terraces create a successive hollowing out of the volume, culminating in the sharp corner of the curved block, while an articulation of double vertical elements on the short side of the orthogonal part point to the front of the building. However, there is no frontality as in so many other buildings by Mario Botta. This front is no longer one that relates the building to the outside world, to the distant view, or to the street. It is not a front to be seen, but only to be experienced. It has to do with the way one approaches the main entrance, with the way one enters. The gesture remains discreet. The composition of the two volumes does not need a strong facade; its presence is solid. A serene place, the building can address its surroundings without losing its sense of subtle monumentality and spatial quality.

View of the two apartment buildings from the town. Facing page: detail of the metal roofing extending outward from the cylindrical volume of the stairs connecting the two levels.

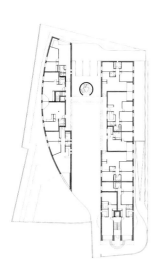

The covered courtyard; view of the balconies;
first floor plan

Museum for Modern and Contemporary Art and Cultural Center

Rovereto, Italy, 1988-1993/2001

This Museum and Cultural Center in Rovereto has the character of an urban intervention woven into the existing fabric. Mario Botta succeeds not only in integrating the old and the new in terms of use, but also in creating a large complex that does not impose its size on the scale of its urban surroundings. "In a sense, the overall design was generated from control of spaces rather than individual building design, from 'voids' rather than 'solids,' from the negative rather than the positive,"[2] he recalls.

The strong independent presence of the museum is not revealed at first sight. Its impressive mass remains partially hidden underground. Two palaces on Corso Bettini give a front to the building. A small alley between them forms an axis that leads to the central courtyard. This spacious public piazza, in the shape of a circle, becomes the heart of the complex and connects to the public space developed at the back of the palaces and the street.

The museum expands its uses to include the two palaces connected to them on the basement and ground levels. Architecture and book museums, a reading room with a top lit by a pyramidal skylight, and the museum storerooms are placed in the basement. The spacious piazza gives access to the museum, the cafeteria, the restaurant and the bookshop. The large exhibition hall and the audio-visual rooms are located on the first level, while the second floor houses exhibition spaces. Circulation through the galleries on the two upper floors takes place around the central courtyard, while staircases occupy the end corners of a square that is formed around it. Ample light comes from above through a series of skylights that give form to the roof.

What takes place underneath is only exposed by means of skylights or sunken courtyards. The actual size of the building is not properly revealed. It is, instead, carefully balanced so that what is revealed is in proportion to the existing buildings. Then, on the first and second floors, the museum becomes an orthogonal volume emptied out to create the circular courtyard of the central core. Its form acquires geometrical presence. Open only on the first level, with a colonnade, the building has no other openings. The elegant proportions of the two palaces define the front on the street, while the new facade at the back, clad in *pietra dorata*, chooses to remain silent. It is the central piazza that attracts all the attention, crowned as it is by its distinctive metal structure. Even though the spatial organization is complex, the central courtyard creates a point of reference.

The way the building relates to the city, the transition from the public space to the interior, the process of entering and its movement, as well as the ability to understand the spatial structure, are important in the design of the museum. The hidden mass and the gradual disclosure of the geometricity of the building shows the formation of the volume. The acquired facade, the rhythm of the existing openings, and the solidity of the new walls point to the elaboration of the surface and its meaning as a front. The succession from the alley to the courtyard, from the axial passage to the culmination of the centripetal space, and its powerful public presence translate movement and orientation into form. The metal

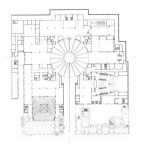 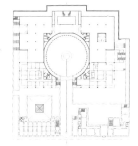 

Plans of the ground, first and upper levels   Model

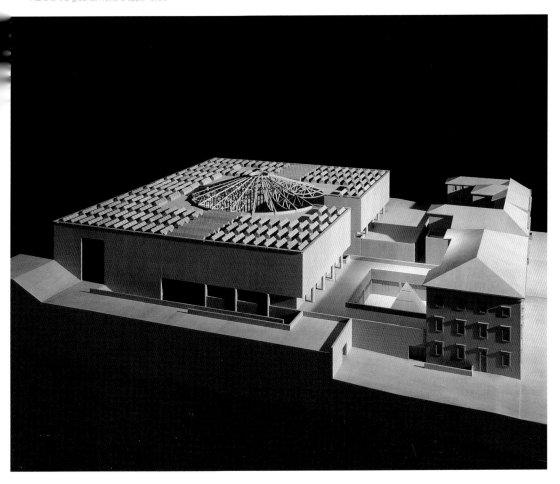

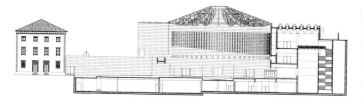

structure of the courtyard
becomes a sign that signifies the
presence of the core. The
museum offers a sensitive
interpretation of existing spatial
relations, its composition a
complex interplay with space
and form.

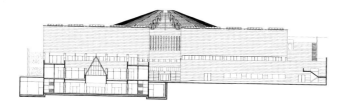

Longitudinal and cross sections

Model; longitudinal section

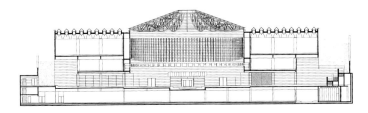

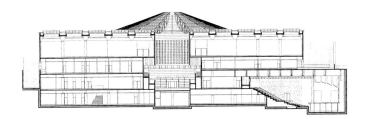

Offices and Housing

Maastricht, Netherlands, 1990-2000

Vast, abandoned industrial areas close to the historic part of a city offer possibilities for the redevelopment of urban structure. A new plan for an area of this kind by the architect Jo Coenen gave the city of Maastricht the opportunity to involve architects Aldo Rossi, Alvaro Siza, Luigi Snozzi, Aurelio Galfetti and Mario Botta in the rejuvenation of the area.

The site assigned to Mario Botta is located at a turning point on the central axis of the new area. It is a triangular lot, one side of which is formed by a street in the residential area and the other by the motorway. The issue of the corner is dealt with by use of a cylinder which, placed in the middle, articulates two linear volumes. The determination of uses is expressed by the volumetric composition, so that apartments are located in the cylindrical volume, while offices are located in the two linear ones. In its tripartite articulation of surface, the design features deep cuts that reveal loggias and an ordered repetition of windows. The cylinder, being almost double the height of the linear volumes, becomes the focus.

A square courtyard is delineated within the cylinder. Once again, negative space takes over the interior. Two large portals in front and a generous cut at the rear reveal the courtyard to the exterior. However, instead of opening up the courtyard to the city, it now opens to the motorway. The boundary of the cylinder at the other side needs to remain uninterrupted, for it shapes the middle element, articulating the corner. The cylinder, greater in scale and distinctive in its treatment of surface, is suspended between autonomy and subversion. If in other cases the cylinder is chosen as an autonomous form in order to be distinct, its shape is now chosen to articulate instead of keeping at a distance. And yet, the difference in size from the linear blocks addresses its primary role. While the linear blocks exist to set a limit, to create a boundary for the site and to frame the perspective, the cylinder remains the center of gravity. Set firmly on the ground, it raises its height to create a focal point for the area.

The antithesis between the massive volume of the cylinder and the linear blocks is further accentuated in the inner part of the composition. The linear facades become transparent at the ground floor level, while they retreat on the third floor, with only the zigzagged outline of the light roof to remind the viewer of their actual height. Suddenly, the end points of the blocks are raised into twin towers. The vertical cuts and the loggias on the top, covered by the transparent roofs, emphasize the monumentality of the whole. The difference in height is partially negated. What started as a play with the elements of the site is now enriched by the potential of a strong monumental image.

Detail of the facade of the central volume

Perspective sketch

Detail of the connection point between the
circular residential volume and the rectilinear
office volume

Facing page: the rear facade of the building is
opened with an internal courtyard oriented
toward the street intersection

Scientific College

Città di Pieve, Italy, 1993-2000

Placed on a steep hill, the college is set on the city limits of a town not far from Perugia, outside the city walls, and close to the church of Sant'Agostino. The building takes the shape of a fan. The front part is composed of three individual units, in the form of a tower divided into two more, each one covered by a slightly cylindrical roof, and connected to the other by its edge. At the back, three more towers are formed, but, this time, staircases occupy the space in between. The backbone, the internal circulation path, bends and follows the contours of the cliff, while distancing between the towers allows natural light to illuminate the interior from both sides. The towers remain as distinct in plan as they are in volume. The building keeps a distance from the square; a generous gap allows light to enter the lower floors at the back. The entrance and administration area, a small cafeteria and a conference room are located on the third floor, entered from the back on the ground level by means of a bridge that leads into a portico. One floor up and three more down complete the organization of the interior. Classrooms are placed along the front part on all floors and also at the back on the two floors above ground.

The building gives the impression of a fortress the way it stands firmly on the cliff. Its presence defines a limit, delineates the boundary for the spacious new square. The public space between the existing church and the new complex becomes the generator of the design. The site dictates its preferences. The building will shape the cliff; its presence will not compete with the mass of the church. It will be, instead, a strong foundation that retains the steep slope. Its towers become buttresses; the external boundary that wraps around them will play with this image. It expands at the base, and gradually compresses to the body of the building as is comes closer to the top. Distancing of the external envelope from the internal mass will create a front, allowing for exploration of the form.

A tripartite division of base, middle, and upper parts makes each tower an autonomous object. The compactness of their top distinguishes it from the openness of the lower part. The external boundary is, once more, made complete at the base. The elaborate facades of the towers are different from

The building in the landscape

Facing page: two towers characterized by large horizontal openings

their solid side walls; a kind of *brise-soleil* shapes their front. The slight curve of the roofs accentuates the skyline. The reading of the primary volume remains intact. There is no subtraction of the mass, no emptying out of the volume. Void is contained by the external skin; negative space exists only because of its presence. The single front of the early projects by Mario Botta has given way to a surface that wraps around the volume. Accentuation of the front is still a matter of volume; but surface can also claim its part.

All the towers are the same. Differentiation is permitted only in the middle one at the back; the main entrance needs to be signalled. The three towers are each divided into two in elevation; thus, six towers create the front. Their division breaks the scale of the whole. Repetition creates a rhythm, for this is a composition of one element in repetitive order. The breaking up of scale does not hide mass; it creates presence instead. Emphasis is given to the vertical aspect. Volumes stand out in sharp relief. Deep shadows emphasize contours. Then, verticality needs to be counterbalanced by its opposite. The horizontal stripping of the openings creates illusions about the actual number of floors. What takes place inside is not revealed on the outside. A constant play with scale hides the size of the building, enhances monumentality, stability, and the gravity of the vertical element.

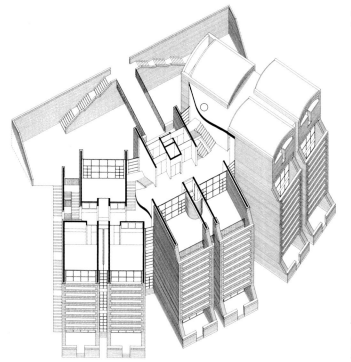

On the previous pages: the eastern frontage with the six towers

Axonometric with the interior layout

Facing page: eastern frontage with three blocks; a walkway connects the street level to the entrance portico

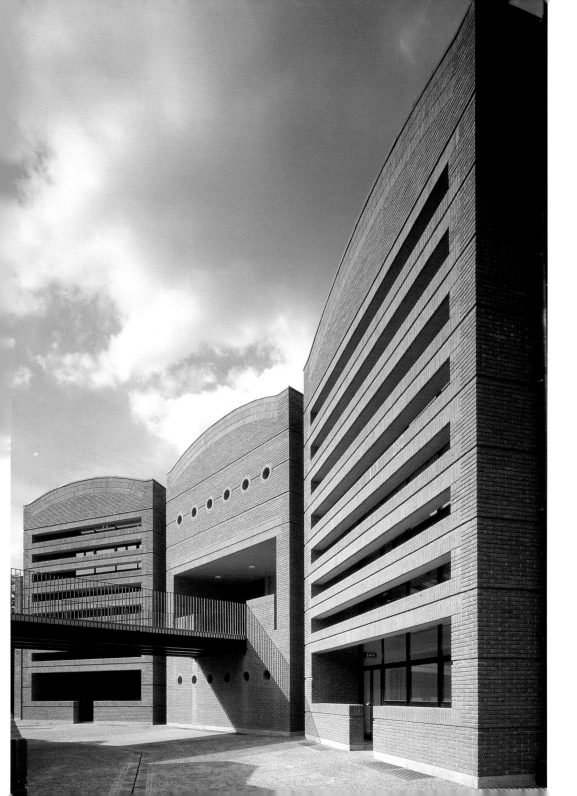

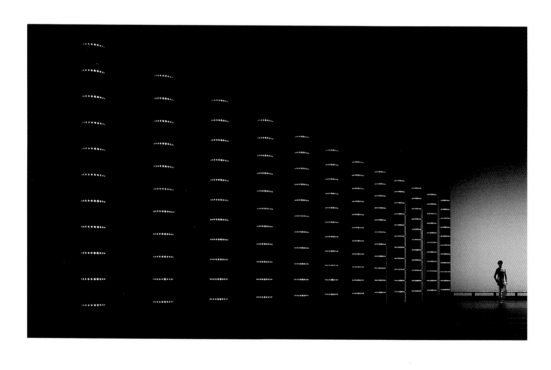

Chapter five

A world of imagination and objects

Mario Botta's Scenographies

Anne-Marie Werner

No matter what field Mario Botta is involved in—architecture, stage architecture or works of design—his artistic creations always bear his unmistakable signature; a style which reveals, to quote Heinrich Klotz, "a considerable degree of self-confidence"[1]. Botta first became occupied with ballet scenery in the early nineties. Initially devoting his attention to the *Nutcracker* in 1992, followed by *Medea* in 1994 (both ballets staged under the choreography of Bernd R. Bienert at the Opernhaus Zurich), Botta later worked on *Ippolito* when it was premiered by Heinz Spoerli at the Basle Stadttheater. It was Bernd R. Bienert, wanting to go beyond mere stage decoration and create "a design for the stage that would have equal status with the music and the choreography"[2], who first brought the architect in contact with "the magic of theater"[3]. Botta was now faced with the opportunities for free artistic expression offered by the stage as well as the conditions, specific to this media, for realizing scenographies.

It is well known that stage sets also contain their own iconographic references based on the narration—whether it be E.T.A. Hoffmann's Christmas tale or ancient myths—which guide the imagination of the architect. The text itself shows nothing, it merely narrates and, at the same time, challenges the architect to subdivide the black box and create a setting for the choreographic interpretation of the different narrative episodes. Although the architect does not invent the contents, he does create the framework within which they can become visible, thus rendering the invisible visible. In *The Nutcracker*, the text suggests the forms whose silhouette is perceived, for example, as the "teeth" of a nutcracker or as the profile of a Christmas tree. In *Medea*, the appearance of the white horse on the stage is inspired by an episode in which Jason gives his son a horse as a present. In *Ippolito* the columns are transformed into a metaphor for a Greek building, conjuring up the original location of the mythological events.

Together with the textual contents underlying the action, the black box of the theater provides the point of departure for the stage design. As we know from psychology[4], a black room is a primal domain forming an emotional foundation for subsequent experiences of space and is, as such, necessarily present in all experience of space. This emotional foundation is not subdivided, and defies all attempts to determine its scale or posit finite boundaries; and unlike the brightly-lit room, the black box cannot be experienced as an opposite. It appears as a purely psychological quality, "penetrating" the psyche in such a way that human beings feel they are at its mercy. Hence, according to Eugene Minkowski, "the ego can be permeated by darkness but not by light. The ego does not assert itself against darkness but blends

Sketch for the set design for the Nutcracker
Suite

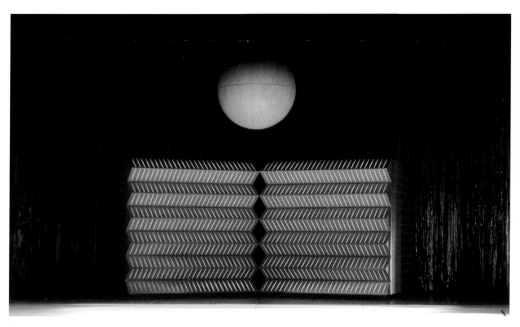

Two positions of the set for the Nutcracker with the two large serrated
wooden blocks and the suspended sphere

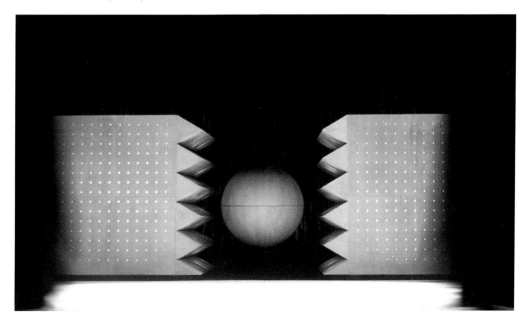

The Nutcracker: a scene from the ballet

with it, and becomes one with it."[5] The black box is shapeless, inhabited by the dimensions of the mysterious, the unknown. It is pure depth, acting as a medium. In addition to its psychological quality, the black box also has a mythical quality. In his "Philosophie der symbolischen Formen," Ernst Cassirer showed that grasping the origin of the Universe as night-space is one of the essential mythical conceptions of the ancients; the first subdivision of this night-space is associated with a "primal phenomenon": the "emergence of light from the night"[6]. In Hesiod's Orphic epic *Theogony*, for example, the original black space is referred to as 'chaos' and it constituted the very origin of the universe. "Verily, first there was chaos and then the earth."[7] Thus, chaos is an immeasurable, dark ground from which matter, the earth (Gaia) and the driving forces (Eros)—which make it possible for the gods to come into being—are derived. The black box of the stage, a room charged with psychological and mythical meaning, is subdivided by light and form in Botta's stage architecture; these subdivisions are, in turn, adopted and taken further in the choreography.

The act of drawing is the first step toward visualizing the division of space with specific formal elements. Botta has done some very impressive designs, whose significance extends far beyond that of preparatory sketches. As the original illustration of an artistic conception, the design is initially directly and intimately related to the concept, thus giving it an eminently intellectual character. Furthermore, it represents the preliminary stage in materializing the scenery and is thus a phase of experimentation, too, one which initially, at least, conveys subjective, personal impulses. Characterized by spirituality and individual spontaneity, Botta's scenery designs are by no means marginal phenomena without any claim to intrinsic artistic value. They combine a "minimum degree of physical existence"—"only" consisting of a few pencil or oil-chalk strokes—with a "maximum degree of conceptual force"[8], thus appearing as a completely valid medium for making an artistic statement. Botta's vocabulary of forms is characterized by its reduction to geometrical ideal forms: the ellipse, the circle, the square and the rectangle. The architect eliminates all secondary details in order to express the essential, thus following on the achievements of the avant-garde. In his book *Toward a New Architecture* of 1923, Le Corbusier stated: "Our eyes are constructed to enable us to see forms in light. Light and shadows reveal the forms; cubes, cones, spheres, cylinders and pyramids are the great primary forms revealed by the light; the image they present to us is pure, tangible, and free from ambiguity. For this reason they are *beautiful forms, the most beautiful there are.*"[9]

In his set designs for the Opernhaus Zurich, Botta's repertoire of forms avails itself of two different registers: one strictly geometrical, the other—its poetic counter-pole—far more flexible and soft, containing elements set in slightly oscillating motion. In *The Nutcracker*, two powerful, angular volumes, as a symbol for the "mathematical-militaristic-masculine" world, and a sphere almost three meters in diameter as the symbol for the "Christian-loving-feminine" world[10] are contrasted with a curtain, made of light-sensitive strips, that can be quickly made to glitter and flutter. In *Medea*, there is a tension between the two quadratic elements: the sphere and the arched form of a transparent bridge

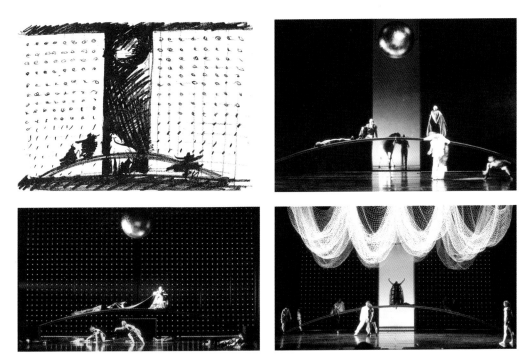

Working sketch for Medea and three moments of the set during the performance

on the one hand, and a moving net recalling cloud formations, a metaphor for the threads of fate, on the other[11]. In *Ippolito*, however, Botta does not restrict himself to simple, isolated elements of sculptural quality that can move within the stage area, but creates an archaic geometrical place of immense depth by virtue of a diagonal colonnade to form a round horizon. Now and then, the elliptical cylinder provides a glimpse through an arched opening onto a staircase, drawing our eyes further into the depths, and dividing the stage into two domains, an inner and an exterior.

Botta radically dismisses the stringency of the modernists—who, by turning their backs on decoration, consistently emphasized the straight, neutral, geometrical surface—and gives his geometrical elements an ornamental character. In his stage architecture, Botta works over the geometrical areas decoratively with perforations and linear incisions. In *The Nutcracker* and *Medea*, the angular volumes and sets are illuminated from within to display regular arrangements of illuminated points on their perforated surfaces. In *Ippolito* he creates illuminated linear structures, and injects rhythm and dynamics into the columns composed of drums. Depending on the way these geometric elements are turned and positioned on the stage, they create a new architectural setting that lends them a variety of meanings. In *The Nutcracker*, for example, the cubes are hung at angles, their serrated edges facing each other. In this position, their negative image creates the profile of a fir-tree; but when the sphere is shown as a positive image between the sides of the teeth, we have the impression of a nutcracker about to crack open a nut. When the cubes hang straight, placed directly alongside one another with the serrated sides

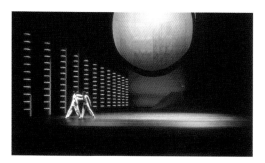 

Set design for Hippolytus: three architectonic elements, the column, the
suspended wooden cylinder and the staircase create the scene, with
magical effects of lighting and projected colors

facing the audience, a large surface is created, rendered dynamic by a herringbone pattern. The sphere
suspended above appears to be a heavenly body. This striking composition showing a lower sphere
determined by horizontal structures that can be mentally extended into infinity, and an upper sphere
occupied by a motionless, circular heavenly body charged with magical force, creates an impression that
can only be described as surreal. Here, I should like to draw the reader's attention to Max Ernst and, in
particular, his oil painting *The Marriage of Heaven and Earth* of 1962, where an earthly realm of
horizontally arranged structures, which become a metaphor for infinity, is distinguished from a heavenly
realm containing a star unfamiliar to us. Hence, Botta's scenography for *The Nutcracker* appears as a
vivid allegory for cosmic, timeless forces springing from a primal, mythical black space, and takes on a
very laconic, archaic character.

In *Ippolito*, a curved horizon is transformed alternately into a starry sky and a moon, likewise symbolizing cosmic harmony. In *Medea*, the recourse to an ancient, mythical body of ideas is brought out even more forcefully by the introduction of the horse. A characteristic of the mythological mind is the creation of unity. In contrast to rational, logical consciousness, which consistently establishes a separation between the human being and a nature that is only accessible at a scientific level, mythical consciousness postulates an immediate identity between the human and natural realms. It does not create any distance, presupposing instead the experience of a unity in which there is no distinct dividing line among the divine, the human, the animal and botanical worlds. In Cassirer's words: "Nowhere in the early stages of the mythical view of the world is there a radical break cutting man off from the totality of all that is living: from the animal and plant kingdoms"[12].

By bringing the horse onto the stage, Botta achieves two things: on the one hand, he makes a reference to the poetry of the libretto and, on the other hand, its appearance conjures up the mythological state of an instinctual, pre-rational unity. Botta follows a similar approach in his architecture. There the tree takes the place of the horse. Botta had a solitary tree planted on the highest point of the "Ransila I" commercial building in Lugano. He tells us that he "fell in love with a tree that reverses the usual rules. It represents nature *on* a work of architecture. There is a tower in Lucca in Italy that has a tree at its highest point. The tree grew there accidentally, but over the centuries, it became magnificent. This is a very lively idea that seems quite different from our usual concept of modernity. There is the question of the relationship of architecture to the sky, which I feel is just as important as its relationship to the ground".[13] The conceptual instruments of modernist and postmodernist architecture fail completely in the face of Botta's project of overturning the rational view of the world. As a link between heaven and earth, architecture is part of an ancient, cosmic vision which unites all that is living in a mythical symbiosis beyond the dogmatic world of reason and its heir, technology. In a word: Botta's realizations both in architecture and on the stage are the incarnation *par excellence* of what Max Ernst referred to as *The Marriage of Heaven and Earth*.

Working sketch for Hippolytus

Guscio

Triennale di Milano, 1984-1985

Another piece of furniture and an object at the same time: it defines a space for two persons sitting face to face. A space for looking at each other, for talking and writing, reading, thinking and lounging. The seasoned beech–slat construction achieves a continuous level of transparency of the surfaces, which also act as the frame, separating the inner space from the exterior one, without isolating it. The shell was meticulously crafted by the Meani brothers, Lissone-based cabinetmakers. It stands as proof of the skill, love, dedication, and pleasure that characterize the work of great craftsmen. (Mario Botta)

Watch

1998-1999

Working sketches and two variants of the
watch for Pierre Junod in stainless steel;
black face and watchband, white face and
steel watchband.

Mia e Tua: wine and water

2000

Micro-architecture for the table for Alessi: Mia e Tua, wine (0.7 lt) and water (1 lt) pitchers in chrome-plated steel

Ceramic vases

1999-2000

Thirteen ceramic vases (1999)
Below, actual-size prototypes in pear wood

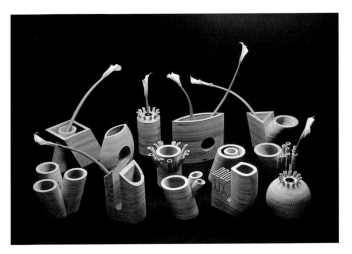

Notes

Introduction

[1] Mario Botta in interview with Gabriele Cappellato, in "Sign, form, design," in *Space: Architect Mario Botta*, p. 41.

[2] For a discussion of the compositional structure of Mario Botta's houses, see I. Sakellaridou, "La Composition Architecturale a-t-elle une structure?" in Pierre Pellegrino (ed), *Figures Architecturales, Formes Urbaines. La Bibliotheque des Formes* (Geneve: Anthropos, 1994), pp. 361-380. In a more extensive discussion, nineteen of his houses are analyzed as a case study for the notion of central concept or 'parti' and the development of an architectural idiom. Three faces are identified which show an evolution of this 'parti' from combinations to structure. The 'parti' is identified as the deep structure of the building, a structure that is abstract, global, and capable of many realizations. See I. Sakellaridou, *A Top-down Analytic Approach to Architectural Composition*, Ph.D Thesis (London: Bartlett School of Architecture, University College, 1994).

[3] For a discussion of the relation between form and meaning in Mario Botta's churches, see I. Sakellaridou, "From the Underlying Formal Structure to the Meaning: Five Churches by Mario Botta," in *Proceedings of VI International Conference of IASS* (Guadalahara Mexico, 1997).

[4] Mario Botta, *Ethik des Bauens. The Ethics of Building*, (Roma-Bari: Gius. Laterza & Figli Spa, 1996; English and German transl., Basel: Birkhauser Verlag, 1997), p. 25.

[5] The issue of logic of composition and of the compositional structure is discussed in I. Sakellaridou, *A Top-down Analytic Approach to Architectural Composition*. See, also, I. Sakellaridou, "The Logic of Architectural Composition," in I.Rauch and G.Carr (eds) *Semiotics around the world: Synthesis in Diversity* (New York: Mouton de Gruyter, 1997), pp. 561-564.

Chapter one

[1] Extract from the project report.

[2] For discussion of design gestures and the convex aspect of the underground building, see A.M.Kotsiopoulos and I. Sakellaridou, "Planning and Resign Reversals: The Experience from a Large Scale Underground Project," in *Underground Structures*, IUASS (Delft, 1992), pp. 242-252. Also for the readability of form of the underground library, see A.M.Kotsiopoulos and I.Sakellaridou, "Underground Ex-tensions. Forms and Implications," in *Proceedings of the International Conference ACUUS on Underground Space '97* (Montreal, 1997).

[3] Pierluigi Nicolin, *Mario Botta. Buildings and Projects 1961-1982*, (New York: Electa Rizzoli, 1984).

[4] The definition *canonic*, in distinction to *pre-canonic* and *post-canonic*, describes that phase in the evolution of the architectural language of Mario Botta in which a stable compositional structure has been established. I. Sakellaridou, *A Top-down Analytic Approach to Architectural Composition*, Ph.D Thesis (London: Bartlett School of Architecture, University College, 1994).

Chapter two

[1] Peter Disch (ed.), *Mario Botta, La ricerca degli anni '80*, (Lugano, 1990).

[2] Philip Jodidio, *Mario Botta*, (Köln: TASCHEN, 1999), p. 58.

[3] Disch, *Mario Botta, La ricerca degli anni '80*.

[4] Disch, *Mario Botta, La ricerca degli anni '80*.

[5] Jodidio, *Mario Botta*, p. 68.

[6] Mario Botta, *Ethik des Bauens. The Ethics of Building*, (Roma-Bari: Gius. Laterza & Figli Spa, 1996; English and German transl., Basel: Birkhäuser Verlag, 1997), pp. 120-121.

[7] Botta , *Ethik des Bauens. The Ethics of Building*, p. 56.

Chapter three

[1] *Foregrounding* is a notion used by the Russian Formalists and is considered the most important function of poetic language denoting the opposite of the automatization that occurs in everyday language. See, J. Mukarovsky, "Standard Language and Poetic Language," ed. and transl. by P. Garvin, in D. Freeman (ed.) Linguistics and Literary Style (Holt Rinehart and Winston Inc., 1970), pp. 40-56., as well as J. Mukarovsky *Structure, Sign and Function: Selected Essays*, ed. and transl. by J. Burbank and P. Steiner (Yale University Press, 1978). The notion is used in an analogy in architecture. For its discussion, see I. Sakellaridou, *A Top-down Analytic Approach to Architectural Composition*, Ph.D Thesis (London: Bartlett School of Architecture, University College, 1994).

[2] Emilio Pizzi, *Mario Botta* (4th updated ed., Barcelona: Editorial Gustavo Gili, S.A., 1997), p. 88.

[3] Rudolph Arnheim, "Notes on Religious Architecture," in *Languages of Design*, 8, vol. 1 (1993), pp. 247-251.

[4] Pizzi, *Mario Botta*, p. 94.

[5] Mario Botta, *Ethik des Bauens. The Ethics of Building*, (Roma-Bari: Gius. Laterza & Figli Spa, 1996; English and German transl., Basel: Birkhauser Verlag, 1997), p. 82.

[6] Mario Botta, "Art and Architecture", in *Mario Botta. Museum Jean Tinguely Basel* (Berne: Benteli Publishers, 1997), p. 108.

[7] Botta, *Ethik des Bauens. The Ethics of Building*, p. 78.

[8] Philip Jodidio, *Mario Botta*, (Köln: TASCHEN, 1999), p. 146.

Chapter four

[1] Mario Botta, *Ethik des Bauens. The Ethics of Building*, (Roma-Bari: Gius. Laterza & Figli Spa, 1996; English and German transl., Basel: Birkhäuser Verlag, 1997), p. 44.

[2] Botta, *Ethik des Bauens. The Ethics of Building*, p. 124.

Chapter five

[1] Klotz H.: Moderne und Postmoderne Architektur, Brunswick/Wiesbaden, 1984, p. 271.

[2] de Raulino, V.: cited in the brochure: Architektur im Bühnenraum, Bernd Roger Bienert inspirierte vier Architekten der Weltelite zu Entwürfen für sein Zürcher Ballett, Mario Botta, Jean Nouvel, Renzo Piano, Aldo Rossi.

[3] Botta, M.: Ethik des Bauens-Ethics of Building, Basle, Boston, Berlin 1997, p.146.

[4] In the following, I refer to the analyses by E. Minkowski.

[5] Minkokwski, E.: Le temps vécu – Etudes phénoménologiques et psychopathologiques, Paris 1963.

[6] Cassirer, P.: Philosophie der symbolischen Formen, Vol. II Das Mythische Denken, 3. Auf. Darmstadt 1958, p. 120

[7] Hesiod: Theogonia, in Hesiod: Translated from the German by Robin Benson.

[8] Schneckenburger, M.: Zeichen zwischen Werkplanung und Utopie, in Ausstellungskatalog Staatsgalerie Stuttgart 1980, p.12

[9] Le Corbusier, Vers une Architecture, Paris, re-edition 1977, p.16 Translated from the French by Robin Benson.

[10] de Raulino, V.: a.a.O.

[11] de Raulino, V.: a.a.O.

[12] Cassirer, P.: a.a.O. p.213

[13] Botta, M. cited in Jodidio, Ph., Stone, Light and Reason, in : Mario Botta, Cologne 1999, p.54.

Mario Botta's Writings

1970

La forma della città, "Corriere del Ticino" [Muzzano], 24 October 1970.

1972

Strutture della città, "Corriere del Ticino" [Muzzano], 11 November 1972.

1976

Altre riflessioni sull'architettura, "Libera Stampa" [Lugano], 30 December 1976.

1970

Extraits du programme-Aperçu des travaux-Postscriptum, "DA Informations", 1977, 10, pp. 1-12 [Ecole Polytéchnique Fédérale de Lausanne].

House at Ligornetto, The Parish House, House at Stabio, House at Cadenazzo, Project for a Residence near Lugano, "GA Global Architecture Houses", 1977, 3, pp. 62-93.

Appunti sui problemi dei centri storici, "Il nostro Paese", 1977, 16, pp. 57-72.

Presentation of my work in Switzerland, "International Laboratory of Architecture and Urban Design", 1977, 1, pp. 54 [1st Residential Course ILAUD].

Un'occasione mancata. Analisi critica del concorso di Tenero, "Rivista Tecnica", 1977, 4, pp. 27-33.

1979

Architecture and "Environnement", "a + u Architecture and Urbanism", 1979, 105, pp. 51-110, [reprinted in "Werk, Bauen + Wohnen", 1980, 1-2, pp. 36-37; P. Nicolin, F. Chaslin Mario Botta 1978-1982 Laboratoire d'architecture, catalogue de l'exposition, Electa-Moniteur, Milano-Paris 1982, pp. 115-116; in Dopo l'Architettura Postmoderna, ed. L. Ferrario, Kappa, Roma 1983, pp. 24-28; "Bulletin UIA", 1983, 12].

Transormation and Re-use of a Farmhouse, "GA Global Architecture Houses", 1979, 6, pp. 160-167.

L'artificio e l'illusione. La misura del decoro. Un parametro alla natura, "Gran Bazaar", 1979, 3, pp. 77.

Un recinto di architettura, "Gran Bazaar", 1979, 4, pp. 192-197.

1980

Casa unifamiliare, "AD Architectural Design", 1980, 5-6, pp. 103-106.

Il disegno, il luogo e il progetto, in Var. Am Rand des Reissbretts. 10 Schweizer Architekten, hg. R. Brosi, Ausstellungskatalog, Studio 10, Chur 1980.

Werkstätten in Balerna, "Archithese", 1980, 1, pp. 46-47.

Residence near Lugano Ticino, Switzerland, "GA Global Document. Special Issue 1970-1980", 1980, 1, pp. 84-85.

L'ultimo progetto di Le Corbusier, in Le Corbusier. La ricerca paziente, ed. S. Pagnamenta, B. Reichlin, Exhibition catalog, Federazione Architetti Svizzeri - Gruppo Ticino, Lugano 1980, pp. 139-150; [reprinted in Le Corbusier Krankenhausprojekt für Venedig, hg. W. Fuchs, R. Wischer, Dietrich Reimer Verlag, 1980, pp. 7-8].

Progetti per la città, progetti contro la cilttà, "Lotus International", 1980, 25, pp. 108-110.

Une maison familiale encore, "Werk, Bauen + Wohnen", 1980, 5, pp. 18-20.

1981

Maison unifamiliale. Pregassona, Suisse, "L'Architecture d'aujourd'hui", 1981, 213, pp. 102-106.

L'albero come eccezione, "Lotus International", 1981, 31, pp. 37-40.

Centro delle scienze a Berlino, "Rivista Tecnica", 1981, 10, pp. 42-48.

Uno spazio per Guernica, "Rivista Tecnica", 1981, 10, pp. 49-51.

Palestra comunale a Balerna, "Rivista Tecnica", 1981, 11, pp. 40-43.

Introspezione della casa, "Ville Giardini", 1981, 159, pp. 2-7.

Alvaro Siza, "Werk, Bauen + Wohnen", 1981, 4, pag. 10 [reprinted in german] Sach-Gedicht, gegenständlich, "Hochparterre", 1989, 5, pag. 5.

Ein Raum für "Guernica", "Werk, Bauen + Wohnen", 1981, 11, pp. 4-5.

Postface. Le mur et la lumière, in Ando by / par Ando, par. F. Labbé, S. Salat, Arc en rêve, Bordeaux 1981, 54.

Mario Botta, A propos Internationale Bauausstellung Berlin, "Dortmunder Architekturhefte", 1981, 16, pp. 20-21.

1982

Botta Collection. Prima e Seconda, in Alias, Milano 1982 [company catalog].

Construire pour la ville, "AMCCS" [Chambéry], 1982, 5.

Bauen für die Stadt, in Var. Freiburger Staatsbank, Freiburger Staatsbank, Freiburg 1982, pp. 36-41.

Guernica, in Var., Vergangenheit-Gegenwart-Zukunft, hg. T. Osterwald-Vowinkel-F.Werner, Ausstellungskatalog, Würtembergischer Kunstverein, Stuttgart 1982, pp. 222.

Projet pour la Maison de la Culture de Chambéry, "Le carré bleu", 1982, 1, pp. 21-23.

Nota, in Mario Botta. La casa rotonda, ed. R. Trevisol, L'Erba Voglio, Milano 1982, pp. 90-91.

Casa a Stabio, "Rivista Tecnica", 1982, 2, pp. 34-37.

Progetto per la "Maison de la Culture" a Chambéry, "Rivista Tecnica", 1982, 11, pp. 55-63.

1983

Science Centre, "AD Architectural Design", 1983, 1-2, pp. 64-65.

Botta Collection. Terzo, in Alias, Milano 1993 [company catalog].

Per saldare un debito di riconoscenza, "Cenobio", 1983, 3, pp. 195-201.

Giardino Urbano. Houston Commentary, "Domus", 1983, 639, pp. 2-5.

Centro delle Scienze a Berlino, "Parametro", 1983, 121, pp. 34-36.

Das Projekt für die Freiburger Staatsbank, "Werk, Bauen + Wohnen", 1983, 1-2, pp. 29-30.

1984

Botta Collection. Quarta, in Alias, Milano 1984 [company catalog].

L'antichità del nuovo, in Architettura del presente e città del passato, a cura di U. Siola, Shakespeare & Company, Brescia 1984, pp. 47-61.

Costruire una banca è costruire una città, "Giornale del Popolo" [Lugano], 18 February 1984.

Alcune note sul restauro di Castelgrande a Bellinzona nel progetto dell'architetto Aurelio Galfetti, "I nostri monumenti storici. Bollettino per i membri della Società di Storia dell'Arte in Svizzera ", 1984, 4, pp. 471-477.

Quale futuro ?, "Interni", 1984, 346, pp. 62-65.

In Ticino è oramai una colpa possedere un sapere ..., "Libera Stampa" [Lugano], 21 March 1984.

Die Bedeutung des Ortes in der Architektur, in Mario Botta. Bauten und Projekte, hg. P. Nicolin, Deutsche Verlags-Anstalt, Stuttgart 1984, pp. 13-15.

Geometrie-Sprache der Menschen, "md Moebel Interior Design", 1984, 2, pp. 17-23.

Quarta, "md Moebel Interior Design", 1984, 11, pp. 54-55.

Un tavolo e tre sedie, "Rivista Tecnica", 1984, 11, pp. 45-49.

1985

L'arcaicità del Nuovo, in James Stirling, Michael Wilford and Associates, La nuova Galleria di Stato a Stoccarda, ed. M. Zardini, Quaderni di Casabella 1, Electa, Milano 1985, pp. 6-7.

La città divisa sulla "multiuso", "Libera Stampa" [Lugano], 20 August 1984.

Importanza della presenza di Sartoris, [Interview with Mario Botta by P. Bodega-L. Delll'Oro], in Var. Alberto Sartoris architetture 1920-1985, Edizioni Grafiche Stefanoni, Lecco 1985, pp. 51-52.

1986

Mario Botta, in AA.VV. L'isolato di Messina, catalogo della mostra, Medina, Cefalù 1986, pp. 28-30 [I Simposio Internazionale di Progettazione, 21 - 29 March 1985, 24 January - 9 February 1986 Messina].

Spazi osceni in luogo pubblico, "Giornale del Popolo" [Lugano], 22 August 1986.

Mario Botta, in Ridisegnare Venezia, ed. T. Quaglia - G. Polli, exhibition catalog, Marsilio, Venezia 1986, pp. 53-55.

Mario Botta, "Notiziario Ordine degli architetti della Provincia di Reggio Emilia", 1986, 3, pp. 7-14 [lecture transcript].

1987

Una ricerca in corso, in Incontri di Architettura, ed. U. Siola - R. Amiante, Guida Editori, Napoli 1987, pp. 77-88.

Sostituzione edilizia sull'area dell'ex Albergo dei Poveri, in Progetti per Napoli, ed. G. Alisio - A. Izzo - R. Amirante, Guida Editori, Napoli 1987, pp. 93-98.

Un progetto per riproporre la lotta atavica tra l'uomo e la montagna, "Valmaggia Viva", 25 April 1987, pag. 3 [Edizione Speciale].

Chiesa di S. Giovanni Battista a Mogno Fusio, "Rivista Tecnica", 1987, 9, pp. 59-65.

Mezzo secolo di speranze, "Eco di Locarno" [Locarno], 26 September 1987.

"Ce passé qui fut mon seul maître", "Quadrangolo" [la domenica del Quotidiano], 13 December 1987, pp. 9-11.

Mario Botta, in Eine neue Galerie für die Sammlung Thyssen-Bornemisza / A new Gallery for the Thyssen-Bornemisza Collection, Collection Thyssen-Bornemisza, Edizione Electa, Milano 1987.

1988

Il dissenso è tempestivo, il consenso arriva tardi, " Popolo e Libertà" [Lugano], 30 January 1988.

The past in present Terms: An Architect's View, "World Link", March 1988, pp. 98-99.

I segreti del giovane Jeanneret, "Costruire", March 1988, pp. 154-155.

I piani regolatori sono strumenti nefasti, "Quotiano" [Bioggio], 25 March 1988.

He incarnated architecture - Mario Botta talks about Le Corbusier, "Passages - Passagen", 1988, 5, pag. 22 [trad. Corbu? L'architecture faite homme, entretien avec Mario Botta par F. Blaser].

Le ragioni dell'architettura e il disimpegno dell'edilizia, "Quotidiano" [Bioggio], 28 July 1988.

Objets récents, "Zeitschrift für Schweizerische Archäologie und Kunstgeschichte", 1988, Band 45, 1, pp. 43-49.

Malissimo il trasferimento al Fevi, "Eco di Locarno" [Locarno], 18 August 1988.

Locarno e il suo festival: quale consapevolezza dello straordinario evento ?, "Quotidiano" [Bioggio], 18 August 1988.

Locarno e il suo festival: la città, il sacro e il profano, "Quotidiano" [Bioggio], 18 August 1988.

Progetto per l'area del Vallone S. Rocco, in Sotto Napoli - idee per la città Sotterranea, ed. V. M. Lampugnani, Electa, Napoli 1988, pp. 80-85.

Il disegno dell'architetto e l'opera di architettura, in Mario Botta, Studi preliminari per la Banca del Gottardo a Lugano, Edizioni A. Salvioni & Co., Bellinzona 1988.

The Church of Mogno-Fusio, "Perspecta", 1988, 24, pp. 78-90.

1989

Aurelio Galfetti: Il mestiere dell'architetto, in Aurelio Galfetti, ed. Xavier Güell, Editorial Gustavo Gili, Barcelona 1989, pp. 6-8.

Eine Bank und Ihre Stadt, "Luzerner Neueste Nachrichten" [Luzern], 27. April 1989.

La construction des objets, in Mario Botta - Construire les objets, par J. P. Felley - O. Kaeser, catalogue de l'exposition, Fondation Louis Moret, Martigny 1989, pag. 7.

I miei ultimi progetti, "Bollettino - Ordine degli architetti della Provincia di Ravenna", September 1989, pp. 11-17 [lecture transcript, 15 April 1989].

Projet pour la cathédrale d'Evry, "Werk, Bauen + Wohnen", 1989, 12, a 64-65

L'Architecture réligeuse et le retour du Monumental, Editeur Epevry, Paris 1990, a pp. 193-198 [Actes des Rencontres Internationales d'Evry le 20 et 21 septembre 1989].

1990

Grazie ! in Mario Botta - la ricerca negli anni ottanta, ed. P. Disch, ADV Advertising Company, Lugano 1990, pag. 5.

The "measure" of the place, the "transparency" of the wall, the "depth" of the Light, in Tadao Ando Sketches / Zeichnungen, Birkhäuser Verlag, Basel - Boston - Berlin 1990, pp. 9-13.

Letter to Watari-um, in Var. Mario Botta Watari-um Project in Tokyo 1985-1990, Watari-um, Tokyo 1990, pp. 7-9.

1991

Postscriptum, in La tenda / La tente / Das Zelt, with texts by T. Carloni, H. Szeemann, J. Pilet, Edizioni Casagrande, Bellinzona 1991, pp. 70-72.

Mario Botta, in Architecture Now, Edited by Maarten Kloos, Arcam Pocket, Architectures & Natura Press, Amsterdam 1991, pp. 28-29.

Nuove chiese, recenti esperienze, [Atti del Convegno tenutosi a Milano il 30 novembre], Curia Arcivescovile, Milano 1991, pp. 3-19.

Le sculture lignee di Aldo Ferrario, in Aldo Ferrario - Skulpturen - Gemälde - Zeichnungen, Ausstellungskatalog, Städtische Galerie Schwarzes Kloster und Augustinermuseum, Freiburg im Breisgau 1991, pp. 3-7.

Vortrag von Mario Botta, in Der kreative Weg, Hg. v. G. Guntern, Verlag Moderne Industrie - Buchverlag, Zürich 1991, pp. 190-224.

Schizzi di studio, in Mario Botta - Schizzi di studio per l'edificio in Via Nizzola a Bellinzona, Spazio XXI - Arti grafiche A. Salvioni, Bellinzona 1991, pag. 3.

Le città bombardate, in I giorni della Slovenia, Edizioni "e", Trieste 1991, pag. 23.

Statements, in Alberto Giacometti, [catalogue de l'exposition, Musée d'Art Moderne de la Ville de Paris] Imprimerie de l'Indre, Paris 1991, pag. 439.

1992

Mario Botta, Cattedrale di Evry, in Architettura e spazio sacro nella modernità, ed. P. Gennaro, exhibition catalog, Editrice Segesta SpA, Milano 1992 pag. 236.

Architetto, uno straordinario "mestiere di speranza", "L'Informatore" [Mendrisio], 31 January 1992.

"Dedicato a mia madre ..." "Vita Nuova", 31 January 1992.

Fede e architettura: un binario plurisecolare, "Popolo e Libertà" [Lugano], 7 April 1992.

Preghiere di pietra, "Azione", 16 April 1992, pp. 6-7 [testimonianza di Mario Botta nell'ambito dell'edizione dei Vesperali 1992].

Per Rino Tami, in Rino Tami, ed. Philippe Carrard - Werner Oechslin -Flora Ruchat - Roncati, exhibition catalog, gta Ausstellungen Departement Architektur, ETH-Hönggerberg, Zurich 1992, pp. 38-39.

Per Giuseppe Mazzariol, in Giuseppe Mazzariol, ed. Chiara Bertola, exhibition catalog, Fondazione Querini Stampalia, Electa, Milano 1992.

Mario Botta, San Francisco "Museum of Moden Art", in Museo d'arte e architettura, ed. M. Kahn-Rossi - M. Franciolli - M. Petraglio, Edizioni Charta, Milano 1992, pp. 150-157.

Testimonianze, in Per Giuseppe Mazzariol, ed. M.Brasatin - W. Dorigo - G. Morelli, Dipartimento di Storia e Critica delle Arti, Università di Venezia - Viella Libreria Editrice, Roma 1992, pp. 36-38.

Studi su Mario Botta [una ricerca fotografica di Giasco Bertoli], Istituto Europeo di Design, Idea Books, Milano 1992, pag. 10.

Ohne Licht, kein Raum, in Lichtfest, Hrsg. Inge Maisch, Ausstellungskatalog, Presse-Druck-und Verlags-GmbH, Ausburg 1992, pag. 63.

Per Jean Petit, in Mario Botta progetto per una chiesa a Mogno, Fidia Edizioni d'Arte, Lugano 1992, pp. 17-21.

1993

La figura dell'architetto oggi, in L'Almanacco 1993, Edizione dell'Almanacco, Bellinzona 1992, pp. 121-123.

Dentro il disegno di Moore, in Henry Moore, Electa Elemond Editori Associati, Milano 1993, pag. 9.

Eine Architekturakademie im Tessin, "Archithese", 1993, 2, pp. 15-19.

Altri cambiamenti, "Lotus", 1993, 77, pp. 108-110.

"Les murs que nous dressons deviendront-ils pas ceux de notre prison ?", "Le Nouveau Quotidien" [Genève], 27 September 1993.

Mario Botta, Ein Zeuge der Hoffnungen, in Hans Bernoulli, Hrsg. K. Und M. Nägeli-Gschwind, Birkhäuser Verlag, Basel-Boston-Berlin 1993, pp. 7-8.

La zattera di pietra, in Pierino Selmoni, ed. M. Bianchi, Quaderni di Villa dei Cedri, Civica Galleria d'Arte, Bellinzona 1993, pag. 9.

Typologie bancaire et morphologie urbaine, in Journée des banquiers 1993, Association Suisse des Banquiers, Bâle 1993, pp. 23-28.

1994

L'immaginario dell'architetto: l'uomo, la casa, il quartiere, in Psichiatria e architettura [Atti del Convegno], ed. C. Molo Bettelini and A. Mazzoleni, Edizione Centro Documentazione e Ricerca dell'Organizzazione Sociopsichiatrica Cantonale - Dipartimento Opere Sociali, Mendrisio 1994, pp. 13-37.

Réflexions sur une nouvelle école d'architecture, "APU-Bulletin", 1994, 1, pp. 7-9.

Mario Botta Farb-Bekenntnisse Zeitgenössischer Architekten, "Daidalos", 1994, 51, pag. 36.

La figura dell'architetto oggi, "Domus", 1994, 7/8, pp. 78-80.

Natur oder Architektur?, "Anthos", 1994, 2, pp. 30-31.

Il sereno Azuma, "Giornale del Popolo" [Lugano], 26 September 1994.

Il progetto architettura Ticino, in L'università della comunicazione, [Atti del Convegno], ed. A. Petralli e S. Vassere, Edizioni Nuova Critica, Canobbio 1994, pp. 13-17.

Quinzaine novembre 1993 Genève, architecture et urbanisme, Institut National Genevois, Nouvelle série des Actes de l'ING, 1994, Livraison 38, pp. 55-70.

Casa brutta, "Micromega", 1994, 5, pp. 40-47.

"Profili in cerchio", in Vittoriano Viganò Una ricerca ed un segno in architettura, a cura di V. Viganò, Electa, Milano 1994, pp. 20-22.

Arazzi, per la SBS e il ristorante parco Saroli a Lugano, in Aoi Huber Il tappeto, Edizioni Tettamanti, Chiasso 1994 and Editions Virgola, Novazzano 1994, pag. 40.

1995

La figura dell'architetto oggi, "Civitas", 1995, 1 / 2 , pp. 9-11.

Projets récents, Conférences Paris d'Architectes et d'Ailleurs, Les mini PA No. 7, Editions du Pavillon de l'Arsenal, Paris 1995, pp. 11-32.

Construire une cathédrale, in B. Delamain La cathédrale de la Résurrection à Evry Premiers instants, Maeght Editeur, Evêché d'Evry, 1995, pp. 4-5.

Cathédral in Evry, "GA Document", 1995, 45, pp. 108- 117.

"Oxford con il lago" Università e comunicazione a Lugano, ed. A. Petralli and S. Vassere, Edizioni Nuova Critica, Lugano 1995, pp. 49-51.

Introduction / Letter by Mario Botta, in Ecuador Monumental, ed. P. M. Durini, Edizione Durini, Quito 1995.

1996

Design and identity, "Louisiana Revy", [exhibition catalog], 1996, 2, pp. 24-25.

Une cathédrale à Evry. Pour Evry, in Mario Botta. La cathédrale d'Evry, Skira Editore, Milan 1996, pag. 13.

Cinque architetture, in Var., Mario Botta Cinque Architetture [catalogo mostra], Skira Editore, Milano. 1996.

Var., La tradizione e la Cultura della Casa nell'alto padovano [Prefazione], Lions Club Camposampiero, Padova 1996.

L'università Ticinese e la Regio Insubrica, "La Regio Insubrica" Circolo Cultura Insieme, Chiasso October-November 1995, pp. 77 - 83.

Segno di speranza per l'uomo d'oggi, "Giornale di Locarno" [Locarno], 29 August 1996.

Art and Architecture, in Museum Jean Tinguely [The Collection], Museum Jean Tinguely and Benteli Publishers Ltd, Bern 1996, pp. 273-280 (German, French and English Edition).

Kunst und Architektur, "B wie Basel", November 1996, pp. 25-30.

P. Bucher, M. Schorer, The Ninth Ticino's University is open, "Vision", December 1996, pp. 2-5 (also in German).

L. Villani, Architettura e natura, "Modo", 1996, 170, pp. 19 - 21.

1997

A cube on the ocean, in D.A. Fatouros & L. Papadopoulos Provoking new identities between sea and city, Nai Publishers, Thessaloniki, 1997, pp. 62-63.

Una mostra di architettura, in Mario Botta Emozioni di pietra [exhibition catalog], Skira Editore, Milano 1997, pp. 34-36.

Il ruolo del "tempio" nella città contemporanea, in La Bibbia per la Famiglia [Supplemento No. 2 a Famiglia Cristiana], ed. G. Ravasi, Periodici San Paolo Editore, Milano 1997, pag. 132.

Museo Jean Tinguely a Basilea, "Rivista Tecnica", 1997, 9 / 10, pp. 7 - 19.

1998

Sculture in città, in Nag Arnoldi [exhibition catalog], Skira Ediotre, Milano 1998, pag. 19

Vivere da architetti, in Le case dell'uomo: Luca Gazzaniga & Carlo Ceccolini [exhibition catalog], Edizioni Clean, Napoli 1998, pag. 1.

Il disegno, il luogo e il progetto, "Disegnare", 1998, 15, pp. 5-8 [da: Am Rande des Reissbretts. 10 Schweizer Architekten, hg. R. Brosi, [Ausstellungskatalog], Studio 10, Chur 1980.]

1999

Une nouvelle figure de l'architecte, in Pour une école de tendance mélanges offerts à Luigi Snozzi, a cura di P.-A. Croset, Presses polytechniques et universitaires romandes, Lausanne 1999, pp. 67-71.

Appunti sulla rappresentazione lignea del San Carlino a Lugano, in Borromini sul lago, a cura di G. Cappellato, Università della Svizzera Italiana, Accademia di architettura Mendrisio - Skria Editore, Ginevra-Milano 1999, pp. 13-18.

Le Corbusier Photographs by Renée Burri/Magnum, Edited and with texts by A. Rüegg, Birkhäuser Publishers, Basel-Boston-Berlin 1999, pag. 11.

Abitare e vivere di più, "Corriere della Sera" (Milano), 11 aprile 2000

Bibliography

Italo Rota, Mario Botta. Architettura e progetti negli anni '70 [with essays by E. Battisti and K. Frampton], Electa, Milano 1979.

Jorge Glusberg, Mario Botta, Centro de Arte Y Comunicacion, Buenos Aires 1980.

Pierluigi Nicolin-François Chaslin, Mario Botta 1978-1982. Laboratoire d'architecture. Electa, Paris-Milano 1982.

Roberto Trevisiol, Mario Botta. La casa rotonda [with text by E. Sanguineti, G. Basilico, A. Sartoris, P. Nicolin, R. Krier and J.M. Reiser], L'Erba Voglio, Milano 1982, l'Equerre, Paris 1982, Gustavo Gili, Barcelona 1983.

Pierluigi Nicolin, Mario Botta Buildings and Projects 1961-1982, Electa/ Rizzoli, New York 1984.

Alberto Sartoris, On the architectural drawing by Mario Botta in Mario Botta. Preliminary Studies, GA Global Architecture Gallery, Tokyo 1984.

Christian Norberg-Schulz-Mirko Zardini, Mario Botta, GA Global Architecture Architect 3, A.D.A., Tokyo 1984.

Virgilio Gilardoni, Gli spazi dell'uomo nell'architettura di Mario Botta, Archivio Storico Ticinese, Bellinzona 1984.

Francesco Dal Cò, Mario Botta. Architetture 1960-1985, Electa, Milano 1985; Electa Moniteur, Paris 1985; Rizzoli, New York 1986.

Francesco Dal Cò, Architecture of Mario Botta, "a+u Architecture and Urbanism" 9, Tokyo 1986 [extra edition].

Stuart Wrede, Mario Botta [exhibition catalog],The Museum of Modern Art, New York 1986.

Mario Botta - Une architecture - trois habitats [catalogue d'exposition, avec des textes de C. Ritschard, J. Baratelli, P. Thomé, V. Mangeat, A. Sartoris et B. Zumthor], Ecole des Arts Décoratifs, Genève 1987.

Peter Pfeiffer, Mario Botta Designer, Corus, Wohlen-Milano 1987.

Mario Botta, "Techniques & Architecture" 377, Paris 1988 [numéro monographique avec des essays de A. Péllissier, J.F. Pousse, M.C. Loriers, F.H. Jourda, G. Perraudin].

Benedetto Gravagnuolo, Mario Botta, Studi preliminari per la Banca del Gottardo a Lugano [exhibition catalog], A. Salvioni, Bellinzona 1988.

Jean Paul Felley et Olivier Kaeser, Mario Botta - Construire les objets. Oeuvre design 1982-198 [catalogue d'exposition], Fondation Louis Moret, Martigny 1989.

Francesco Dal Cò, Mario Botta. Una casa [exhibition catalog with essays by Vittorio Fagone], Electa, Milano 1989.

Jean Claude Garcias, La cathédrale du XXIème siècle, "Art sacré le Renouveau" numéro spécial de "Beaux Arts", Paris 1990.

Peter Disch, Mario Botta. La ricerca negli anni ottanta, ADV Advertising Company, Lugano 1990.

Etsuko Watari, Mario Botta. Watari-um Project in Tokyo 1985-1990, Watari-um, Tokyo 1990.

Giovanni Pozzi, Mario Botta, at the crossroads of culture, "Approach", Osaka, winter 1990.

Emilio Pizzi, Mario Botta. Architectures 1980-1990 [catalogue d'exposition, avec introduction de Werner Oechslin et un entretien conduit par Pierluigi Nicolin], Editorial Gustavo Gili, Barcelona 1991; Artemis, Zürich-München 1991.

Emilio Pizzi, Mario Botta. Obras y Projectos/Works and projects, Editorial Gustavo Gili, Barcelona 1991-re-printed 1997; ed. German/French, Mario Botta, Birkhäuser Verlag, Basel-Boston-Berlin 1991-überarbeitete Neuauflage 1998; ed. Ital., Mario Botta, Zanichelli, Bologna 1991; ed. Port., Mario Botta, Livraria Martins Fontes Editora Ltda., Saõ Paulo 1994.

Tita Carloni, Jacques Pilet and Harald Szeemann, Das Zelt-La tente-La Tenda, Casagrande, Bellinzona - Artemis, Zürich 1991.

Jean Petit, Mario Botta- progetto per una chiesa Mogno/projet pour une église Mogno, Fidia Edizioni d'arte Lugano 1992, id. Engl/Dt ed.

Rolando Bellini, Mario Botta. Architetture 1980-199, Artificio, Firenze 1992.

Emilio Pizzi, Mario Botta, Das Gesamtwerk, Band 1 1960-1985, ed. Engl.: Mario Botta, The complete works, Volume 1 1960-1985, Birkhäuser Verlag, Basel-Boston-Berlin1993; ed. Ital., Mario Botta, Opere complete, volume 1 1960-1985, Federico Motta, Milano 1993.

Rafaella Baraldi, Mario Fiorucci, Mario Botta- Architettura e Tecnica, Clean, Napoli 1993.

Sergio Polano, Under the sign of Aries: new directions in Mario Botta's architectural research, "A+U Architecture and Urbanism" 279, Tokyo 1993.

Jean Petit, Traces d'architecture - Botta, Fidia Edizioni d'Arte, Lugano - Bibliothèque des Arts, Paris 1994.

Emilio Pizzi, Mario Botta. Das Gesamtwerk Band 2 1985-1990, Engl. ed.: Mario Botta, The complete works volume 2, 1985-1990, Birkhäuser Verlag, Basel-Boston-Berlin 1994; ed. Ital., Mario Botta Opere complete volume 2 1985-1990, Federico Motta, Milano 1994.

Mario Botta, Enzo Cucchi La cappella del Monte Tamaro (The chapel of Monte Tamaro), with texts by Fulvio Irace, Ursula Perucchi-Petri and Giovanni Pozzi, Umberto Allemandi & C., Torino 1994 [reprinted 1996].

Mario Botta. Il Museo d'Arte Moderna e Contemporanea di Trento e Rovereto, Skira Editore, Milano 1995.

Fabiola Lopez Duran, Cuatro temas para cuatro maneras de hacer arquitectura in Un lugar, cuatro arquitectos [exhibition catalog], Museo de Bellas Artes, Caracas 1995.

Mario Botta.La cathédrale d'Evry, Skira Editore, Milan 1996 [reprinted 2000].

Mario Botta. Cinque architetture [exhibition catalog with texts by Christian Norberg-Schulz, Giovanni Pozzi, Gabriele Cappellato], Skira Editore, Milano 1996.

Mario Botta vu par Pino Musi, Introduction/Einführung Fulvio Irace, Daco-Verlag, Stuttgart 1996.

Mario Botta. Etica del costruire, ed. Benedetto Gravagnuolo, Editori Laterza, Bari 1996; Dt./Engl. Mario Botta. Ethik des Bauens-Ethics of building, Birkhäuser Verlag für Architektur, Basel-Boston-Berlin 1997.

Philippe Jodidio, Musée Jean Tinguely [numéro spécial de] "Connaissances des Arts", 1996, 98, pp. 8-17.

Mario Botta - Mario Merz im Gespräch mit Marlies Grüterich, hg. Cristina Bechtler, Kunsthaus Bregenz, Cantz Verlag, Ostfildern-Ruit [Stuttgart] 1996.

Mario Botta Emozioni di pietra [exhibition catalog with texts by Benedetto Gravagnuolo, Cesare de Seta, Aldo Masullo, Werner Oechslin, Gabriele Cappellato, Mario Botta], Skira Editore, Milano 1997 [Ed. Engl./ed. Span. Mario Botta Public Buildings, Skira Editore, Milan 1998].

Emilio Pizzi, Mario Botta Gesamtwerk, Band 3 1990-1997, Engl. ed.: Mario Botta, The complete works, volume 3 1990-1997, Birkhäuser Verlag, Basel-Boston-Berlin 1997; ed. Ital. Mario Botta Opere complete 1990-1997, Federico Motta Editore, Milano 1997.

Mario Botta Museum Jean Tinguely [mit Texten von R. Ingersoll, U. Jehle-Schulte Strathaus, J. Y. Mock, S. Polano, N. de Saint Phalle, L. Windhöfel], Museum Jean Tinguely, Basel - Benteli Verlag, Bern 1997.

Philip Jodidio, Mario Botta, Benedikt Taschen Verlag, Köln 1999.

Borromini sul lago, Mario Botta La rappresentazione lignea del San Carlo alle Quattro Fontane a Lugano, ed. Gabriele Cappellato [with texts by Edoardo Sanguineti, Mario Botta, Carlo Bertelli, Giuseppe Panza di Biumo, Arduino Cantafora, Stanislaus von Moos, Nicola Emery, Georges Abou-Jaoudé], Skira Editore, Milano-Ginevra 1999.

Mario Botta La chiesa di San Giovanni Battista a Mogno, [with an essay by Giorgio Cheda], Associazione Ricostruzione Chiesa di Mogno, Mogno-Fusio - Skira Editore, Ginevra-Milano 1999.

Mario Botta. Modelli di architettura (in an essay by Werner Oechslin), Centro Studi dell'abitare Oikos. Bologna 200, Alinea Editrice, Firenze 2000.

La chathédrale de la Résurrection d'Evry, par Emma Lavigne, Editions du Patrimoine, Paris 2000.

Films—media

Senza luce, nessun spazio, by Andreas Pfäffli, Al Castello SA, 1987.

Mario Botta architect, contemporary architects and designers, Victory Interactive Media SA, Lugano 1994. [CD-ROM]

SFMOMA - Un occhio per la città, by Matteo Bellinelli Televisione della Svizzera Italiana, Lugano 1995.

Licht nach innen - Die neuen Bauten des Mario Botta ein Film von Birgitta Ashoff, Bayerischer Rundfunk , München 1995.

Mario Botta, von Charlotte Kerr Dürrenmatt, On Line Video 46 AG, Zürich 1996 für Süddeutscher Rundfunk Stuttgart.

Meta-Mecano, ein Film von Ruedi Gerber Zas Film AG, Zürich 1997.

Tamaro - Pietre e Angeli, Mario Botta, Enzo Cucchi, film by Villi Hermann, Imago film, Lugano, 1998.